THE FAMILY STORE

Susan Harrison McMichael was born and raised in Arizona. She has worn various career hats – English teacher, librarian, business owner, paralegal, and resume writer. For over thirty years she worked in the family store, the office supply store that forms the setting for this book.

Best Wishes
Susan

Books by Susan Harrison McMichael

Box 7, Black Canyon Stage Route

The Family Store

THE FAMILY STORE

Chandler Stationers, a full-line office supply store

We must have it somewhere.

THE FAMILY STORE

From Behind the Counter of an Old-Fashioned Stationery Store

by

Susan Harrison McMichael

Illustrations by the author

Arizona – Social life and customs – Humor

Printed by CreateSpace, an Amazon.com Company

This book is dedicated to

Mother and Dad,

Heather, Beth, Katie
and Jeff

who stood behind the counter
of THE FAMILY STORE

ACKNOWLEDGMENTS

To my family who stirred the memories and offered acerbic advice as the tales unfolded. To the Mesa Writers' Guild who helped me smooth out the rough spots, picked out the nits, and offered encouragement along the way. Thank you.

CONTENTS

ILLUSTRATIONS

PREFACE

This is the tale of a real store set in a real town, the stories inspired by the real people of Chandler, Arizona. This is also the tale of a family, not merchants by education or inclination, but who learned the trade on the fly, made the most of an opportunity, and struggled valiantly to maintain a viable business in a rapidly changing world.

This book is written as a memoir but is really short vignettes of life in a small town. I took the liberty of using actual names of select businesses and businessmen in the community to give the setting of my book a sense of time and place. Others are products of my imagination and used fictitiously. Please don't try to assign these characters to real persons, living or dead.

I hope the cartoon illustrations contribute to the levity of the book. I began a cartoon project during the 1980s when I created a cartoon album commemorating my parents' 50th Wedding Anniversary. Several pictures in this book were taken from that album.

Chapter 1

SWEETIE, IT'S TIME TO RETIRE

"Well, Sweetie," Dad contended. "It's a hoppin' little joint."

"I will *not* be a barmaid!" Mother stomped her foot. Two deep parentheses punctuated her brow. She was obviously rejecting Dad's interest in purchasing a neighborhood tavern.

". . . and *don't* even think about that City Grill!" Mother continued. Neither would she be chief cook and bottle washer at an all-night diner that was on Dad's radar.

These occupations did not fit the image of Dignified Club-Woman that Mother espoused. President of the Washington Women's Club, esteemed member of the P.E.O. Sisterhood, Election Day poll worker, Mother was the epitome of class. A slightly harried woman, thick of waist and grey of hair, Mother juggled her own varied projects with Dad's enterprises.

Dad was a highway engineer who had spent the bulk of his career building roads and bridges across Arizona. As the owner of a small construction company he worked from a dining room table spread with rolls of highway plans or from the tailgate of a pickup truck. Under a haze of Lucky Strike smoke he scribbled long columns of figures on yellow legal pads referring frequently to a slide rule that he carried in a holster on his belt.

Sweetie, Dad's endearing name for Mother, was his general step-n-fetch-it – secretary, bookkeeper, scheduler, parts manager, delivery gal. Living and working with Dad had been a constant detour over the back roads of Arizona. Mother ran interference between Dad's construction jobs in remote parts of the state and equipment supply stores that provided replacement parts for machinery that was in a constant flux of breaking down.

This intrepid duo, Dad, a bandy-legged go-getter of the West, and Mother, a faded belle from the South, were not strangers to stepping into entrepreneurial waters. At different stages of their marriage, from the Great Depression onward, they had owned a gas station and a chicken farm. Before striking out as an independent contractor, Dad had worked for the Arizona Highway Department, but resigned the day a retirement system was implemented. "I'll be damned if I'm going to be a lame duck, just putting in my time until retirement," he declared. Dad was a lone wolf, a man who would make his way in life without government support.

Now, as they both approached the grand old age of sixty, Dad began looking for a "retirement" endeavor. His notion of retirement was to jump into another business. For months he combed the classified section of the *Arizona Republic* for likely business opportunities and scoped out a few – a gun shop, a tire dealership, a pawn shop, a movie theater, a locksmith shop. His business acumen was enough to steer away from those enterprises.

"You're right, Sweetie, bars and small cafés pop up like clockwork in the classifieds," Dad conceded.

"Obviously not good investments," Mother responded, mollified that she would not have to pull beer-on-tap or flip hamburgers.

Dad's interest was roused one Sunday when he saw an inconspicuous notice wedged between listings for a beauty parlor and an insurance agency.

> *Established office supply store for sale. Chandler, Arizona. Contact . . .*

A small-town office supply store was for sale. This was the first time Dad had seen an ad for such a business. That might imply that an office supply store was generally a successful enterprise.

"Everybody needs pencils and writing tablets," Dad reasoned.

* * *

From his home on the northwestern fringes of metropolitan Phoenix, Dad drove thirty miles as the crow flies to check out the little office supply store. In Chandler he met a man of his own mind, a querulous old newspaper editor.

Lynn Williams and his wife Ann had owned the local newspaper, *The Chandler Arizonan*, since the 1930s. Lynn's weekly column, "Petulant Palaver," kept the local gentry tuned-in to the goings-on in this small farming community south of Phoenix.

As a convenience to the citizens of Chandler, and as an additional perk for the newspaper, the Williams kept a small selection of office supplies for sale in the front office. Otherwise the locals had to drive ten miles to Mesa or twenty miles to Phoenix to get paper and pencils, pens and ink, ledgers and calendars, staplers and paper clips, file folders and index cards.

In time the Williams sold the newspaper to a conglomerate that was snapping up local publications. They moved the office-supply part of the business to a small building on the town square. The spin-off business came to be known as Williams' Stationers, and the inventory expanded: file boxes, desk accessories, pencil sharpeners, drafting supplies, slide rules, paper punches, typewriter ribbon, and packaging tape.

The Williams included some high-end stationery supplies like Cross Pens, Crane Writing Paper, and leather journals. Mrs. Williams appropriated the glass shelves near the door and arranged them with hoity-toity gift items like figurines, crystal vases, and porcelain compotes. They added a rack of greeting cards, a small selection of photo albums, and a few Bibles. To accommodate tourists who stayed at the San Marcos Hotel, regional postcards, souvenirs, and books went onto the shelves. A one-stop-shop for office supplies and gifts.

After thirty years, a series of strokes and generally declining health prompted Lynn Williams to sell the office supply business.

* * *

Dad, a product of small-town Arizona, recognized the old-fashioned ambiance of the little community of Chandler. The tentacles of Phoenix, edging into the hinterlands and nipping at the boundaries of outlying communities, had not yet affected the rural nature of Chandler.

Chandler boasted one of the few classic town squares in Arizona. Most of the dusty rural towns in the state evolved from general stores, two-pump gas stations, and tawdry bars strung along state routes. But Chandler was a planned community, the brainchild of Dr. A. J. Chandler who came to Arizona from Canada in 1887 to be the first Territorial Livestock Veterinarian. Dr. Chandler bought up 18,000 acres of desert land south of Phoenix and began ranching. When his vast acreage became more valuable as real estate than as ranch land, Dr. Chandler began subdividing his holdings into farm-size parcels and selling them off. He reserved the center section for a town site where his vision of an oasis in the desert was fulfilled. The founding of Chandler in 1912 coincided with the year Arizona attained statehood, so the fledgling entities grew up together.

The Chandler town square was patterned after a Spanish plaza. The San Marcos Hotel, grand dame of the desert, commanded the northwest corner. Magenta bougainvilleas clambered up the walls of her mission-style architecture. Small businesses shaded by a sidewalk portico lined the colonnade. The park in the center of the square with green grass, mature shade trees, and park benches provided respite to shoppers and travelers who often stopped for a bit of relaxation and refreshment.

The little stationery store was nestled between a café and a haberdashery on the west side of the colonnade.

* * *

Mother and Dad stepped in as new owners of the long-established stationery store. The venture seemed to fill a need for both of my parents. The standard business side for Dad and the gifty frou-frou side for Mother. That they knew nothing about the office supply business did not daunt them.

"If you can operate a mechanical pencil, you can operate an office supply store," Dad said.

Chapter 2

INHERITED EMPLOYEES

When Dad bought the store Viktor and Dorcas came with it.

"Of course, I'll keep your current employees on the payroll," Dad had told Mr. Williams as they ironed out the final details of the store transfer. "That is if they want to stay on board."

"Heh-heh-heh," Viktor giggled nervously. He ran his hand over his receding hair line when told that Dad would like for him to remain on staff.

"Certainly," Dorcas consented. She straightened the cameo at the throat of her lace collar.

Having two seasoned employees on staff would definitely be an asset. Viktor and Dorcas knew the stock in the store. Mother and Dad would not have to flail about looking for file guides or prong fasteners or map tacks, small items tucked into dark recesses on the shelves. Viktor and Dorcas also knew everybody in town. Mother and Dad would get personal introductions to customers as they walked in the door.

"Yes, indeed," said Dad shaking their hands. "You will be the key to a smooth transition. Welcome."

Now that Viktor and Dorcas were assured that their jobs were not on the line, they set about to train the new owners in the fine art of merchandising.

Viktor, a gimpy little chap, looked much older than his forty-some years. In addition to thinning hair, coarse skin, and coke-bottle glasses Viktor suffered from a complicated assortment of allergies that made him the archetypal hypochondriac. Dietary allergies – no chocolate, no cucumbers; they upset his stomach. Dermatological allergies – in times of high stress a scaly rash crept up his neck, behind his ears, and into his hair line. Most serious was an asthma condition. Throughout the day Viktor's rasping breath rattled through his lungs like tarpaper fluttering through fan blades.

At intervals he brought out his inhaler, squeezed and gasped, squeezed and gasped; then he was set for another interval of ragged breathing.

Viktor's entire career had been spent working for the Williams. He had gone to work for *The Chandler Arizonan* as a printer's devil as soon as the ink dried on his high school diploma. Twenty-odd years later Viktor was still the all-around go-to guy for the stationery store. He assisted customers, prepared orders, and made deliveries.

Viktor, unfortunately, had a lisp. "Mithter Hawwithon, a dothen thaplers came in thith order. We never order more than thwee. Thall I thend the otherth back?"

"No, Viktor," Dad growled. "We'll keep the staplers. We get a better price if we order by the dozen."

"Yeth thir," Viktor acquiesced. Apparently there were going to be some changes in the business. Not only did Dad order staplers by the dozen, he ordered ring binders, columnar pads, and file folders by the case.

"I thertainly hope that we can thell all thith thuff." Viktor wrung his hands in dismay.

When a spinning rack full of typewriter ribbons arrived Viktor was beside himself. "Oh, Mithter Hawwithon, we only keep the popular ribbonth in thtock. If a cuthtomer wanth another we make a thpethial order."

"We can't make a sale from an empty wagon," Dad declared. "We will try to anticipate what the customer needs." Dad proceeded to fill the display slots with boxes of twin-spool ribbons for Adler, Remington, Royal, Underwood, and Woodstock machines.

Next came the appointment books, composition books, dispatch books, memo books, notebooks, payroll books, sales books, steno books. Nothing arrived in quantities less than a dozen.

"I hope you aren't making a big mithtake," Viktor muttered thinking Dad would not hear.

It seemed as if the new owner was not trainable.

Dorcas, too, had trouble adjusting to the new owners. A woman over the cusp of sixty, Dorcas was set in a predictable routine. She walked to work each morning from her home two blocks south of the store. Her heavy support hose and her sensible shoes with thick crepe soles testified to a prudent woman who dressed for being on her feet all day. Dorcas wore plain gabardine skirts and neat white blouses caught at the throat with costume-jewelry brooches. The brooches were Dorcas's window into extravagance – colored glass, rhinestone, and gold plated whimsies that she had collected over the years. Today those retro pieces would be all the rage.

Every morning after hanging her sweater on a peg in the stockroom, Dorcas addressed the greeting card rack.

"It's like an army of gremlins comes in at night and shuffles these cards," she said as she went to work straightening the display, restocking empty card slots, and matching orphan cards with stray envelopes.

Only when the greeting card line-up was in military order did Dorcas pick up a rag and attack the dust mites on the what-not shelves lined with music boxes, glass slippers, and porcelain figurines.

"What is this?" Docas exclaimed one morning when a delivery man set a parcel inside the door.

"Oh!" exclaimed Mother. "Maybe it is the piggy banks."

"Piggy banks? We've never carried piggy banks," said Dorcas.

"A couple of weeks ago while you were at lunch a salesman came into the store," Mother explained. "The store didn't have any banks. I ordered a display of piggy banks. They are very cute."

The package revealed a whole barnyard of ceramic banks – piggies, cows, rabbits, ducks, lambs, roosters.

"Humpf," sniffed Dorcas. "I'm sure you'll agree that this is an extravagance. I can't imagine that we will have a call for twelve piggy banks. Piggie banks are for children." But, she set about to incorporate the animal farm on the shelves amid crystal compotes and china candlesticks.

While Viktor was nervous and fussy, Dorcas was composed and bossy. Her bossiness snuck up on you coated with sugar. "*I'm sure you'll agree . . .*" was often her opening statement. It almost made you think that you were making the decisions.

"*I'm sure you'll agree* that the Hummel figurines display to better advantage on the middle shelf," Dorcas said as she changed the arrangement that Mother had just put on the top shelf.

"*I'm sure you'll agree* that Taylor Company's albums are more distinguished than Samuels'," she said as she brought a Taylor Company catalog forth to place an order.

"*I'm sure you'll agree* that we only need a small selection of Cross Pens," she said when she saw Dad studying a catalog of fine writing instruments.

"No, Dorcas! I'm not sure that I agree," Dad barked. "We will order the complete line of Cross Pens. We will also order an assortment of Shaeffer pen and pencil sets. And even a few Parker instruments. Quantity purchase. That's the way we'll go."

New owners and inherited employees had a few rough spots to work out.

Chapter 3

MUSICAL STORES

"Mithter Hawwithon, where will we put all thith thtuff?" Viktor scratched his head as he unpacked an assortment of steel cash boxes, posting tubs, and vertical organizers – clunky gun-metal gray desk items that would occupy precious shelf space.

"The manufacturer was having a close-out," Dad grunted by way of explanation. "I got a good deal." But that didn't solve the problem of where to put "all thith thtuff."

"I'm sure you'll agree that it will take us a long time to sell a dozen pad holders," Dorcas proclaimed sagely. "Where will we keep them?"

"The price break is at a dozen. It doesn't make sense to order fewer," Dad replied.

"There'th no woom for the pothtal thcalth:" Viktor.

". . . or these rotary files:" Dorcas.

". . . or the wubber thtamp kith:" Viktor.

Postal scales, rotary files, rubber stamp kits. Dad had filled the little stationery store to the rafters. There was no room for additional merchandise.

As luck would have it, a few months after Mother and Dad took over the stationers, downtown Chandler went through a version of musical chairs – or musical stores, if you will.

J.C. Penney's, located on West Boston Street, the south side of the square, supplied the population of Chandler with underwear, towels, yard goods, work shirts, and overalls. They also had a catalog department where you could order items that the local store did not carry. The store smelled of floor wax and fabric sizing. When you bought a set of muslin sheets at Penney's you watched the clerk write a sales slip, then tuck the slip along with your money into a cup. She pulled a chord that shot cup and money along a wire to the cashier's office on the mezzanine. While the clerk wrapped your purchase, your change was made upstairs. Change and endorsed sales slip shot back via the same path.

Penney's closed the classic emporium soon after we moved onto the square. They moved to a bigger, more modern building at the north edge of town. Maybe that was the precursor of what would come – a testimony to the evolving nature of town centers.

Dave Saba, who operated a successful western wear store, had his eye on the vacated Penney's site. He took his Levis and pearl-buttoned shirts, his boots and belts, his silver buckles, vests, sheepskin-lined coats, and Stetsons. He moved into the larger store and expanded his cowboy gear empire.

That left Saba's vacated store, a prime location in the center of the block on San Marcos Place, to be appropriated by The New Stationers. A generally finer merchandising situation, our sales space would be more than doubled. A large stockroom at the rear of the building assured Dad of room to store that plethora of cash boxes, posting tubs, and vertical organizers that he had procured on close-out. In preparation for the move Dad purchased additional shelving for the new location, increased his buying power, and established lines of credit with major wholesalers in the office supply business.

I was wallowing in my second trimester of pregnancy when I attended a summer gift show in Los Angeles with Mother and Dorcas. I had recently resigned my position as librarian at a neighboring district high school. Back in those days pregnant teachers were hastily cast aside lest the condition be contagious. School districts had not progressed much beyond the days when married ladies were barred from teaching. I didn't really care. I looked forward to being a stay-at-home-mom for three-year-old Heather and our "new one" on the way. When the children were older I planned to return to school either as an English teacher or as a librarian. I looked forward to the gift show as a refreshing change from stamping hall passes and maintaining decorum in the library.

With a flourish of self-importance, Mother registered us for the L.A. Gift Show, a week-long event where retailers from the western states convened to order giftware and seasonal product for their shelves. Official badges that arrived in the mail entitled us to enter all divisions of the gift show as well as to conduct business with the many wholesalers.

Dorcas, Mother, and I popped tidy straw hats over our permed tresses and pulled neat white gloves over our fingers. Armed with inventory lists and wish lists we boarded an economy flight to L.A. and checked into a budget-friendly hotel in the heart of the city.

Never had I seen such falderal. The AEA (Arizona Education Association) Conventions that I had attended during my years as a teacher were nothing like this. Sure, textbook publishers and distributors of school sports equipment had displays at the AEA Convention, and they circulated slick brochures to lure teachers to their products. However, menial classroom educators had little input in school curriculum choices. The AEA Convention was simply a look-see event for the rank-and-file teacher.

In contrast, I found myself a participatory part of the Los Angeles Gift Show. The badge that I wore carried the same credentials as the badges worn by buyers from Macy's, Bullock's, and Marshall Field's. Vendors greeted this trio representing a small stationery store in the farming community of Chandler expansively and courted our patronage. Bowls of candy and nuts beckoned from every stall. Give-aways and small trinkets accumulated in our totes. We tossed our business cards into dozens of fish bowls and wire cages in hopes of winning stupendous prizes – a vacation for two in Hawaii, a set of copper-clad cookware, a giant stuffed unicorn. Who knows what happened to those business cards. They certainly didn't result in prizes for us.

Wholesalers from around the world occupied booths over the entire L.A. Convention Center. The show spread to various hotels in the city; even to the Ambassador Hotel where Senator Robert Kennedy had been assassinated only a month earlier. (Kennedy, on the presidential campaign trail, was shot three times by Palestinian immigrant Sirhan Sirhan after giving a speech; he died of his wounds twenty-six hours later.) Now, wholesalers hawked helium balloons, cuckoo clocks, and Christmas tinsel on the very site where Kennedy fell. How soon the public had forgotten.

So extensive was the array that shuttle busses ran circuits to a multitude of the gift show sites. Dorcas, an old hand at navigating the L.A. Gift Show, had a ready list of suppliers that we should see. Eburling & Ruess presented lead crystal vases and bone china teacups from Europe; Lefton Pacific imported porcelain birds and flowers from the orient; Fenton Art Glass exhibited a collectible line of hand-blown American glass.

"A display of these lovely Coventry teacups," Mother said as we perused the exhibit at the E & R kiosk. She fingered a delicate cup painted with pansies and daffodils. A complete display would give Mother most of the flowers in an English garden – peony, hydrangea, delphinium, hyacinth. ". . . and two of the matching tea pots," she continued. "You don't see china tea pots much any more." Mother was getting the hang of ordering product by the dozen.

Even Dorcas ventured away from ordering penury amounts and suggested, "These luminaries are lovely. They would make a nice addition to Christmas product." She was pondering an assortment of cut-glass vessels shaped like elegant perfume bottles. They were filled with red lamp oil that was wicked to soft flames flickering from their small top openings.

"Yes, we'll take a display," Mother agreed. A display included two each of six different styles. Mother had become expansive.

Then I made a timorous suggestion, "What about these porcelain music boxes?" The music boxes, embellished with colorful flowers, took several attractive shapes – a piano, a heart, an egg, a sweet little watering can. When the lids were raised clear tunes tinkled forth, melodies like *Beautiful Dreamer* and *Clair de Lune*. My favorite was an old-fashioned telephone that played *Let Me Call You Sweetheart* when the receiver was lifted from its cradle.

My parsimonious nature had been tested. Ordering fine gifts and trinkets was pretty heady stuff. Here I had ordered a dozen music boxes.

We spent four days working our way through the gift show, making new contacts, but also being sure to visit wholesalers that were on Dorcas's list. We ordered knick-knacks and bric-a-brac, books and bookends, stationery and desk sets, gift wrap and ribbons. With an eye to Christmas we ordered ornaments, and holiday cards.

"All thith thtuff" would be shipped two months hence. By that time we would be moving into our new location.

"And then, we can stand behind the counter and sell things," said Mother.

Chapter 4

OPEN FOR BUSINESS

"Don't you dare have that baby during the World Series." Dr. Lloyd dismissed me with a nod tucking his stethoscope into the pocket of his starched white coat.

"Don't you dare have that baby during elk season," Jeff sputtered. My ever-loving husband had a coveted permit for the fall elk hunt.

"Don't you dare have that baby during the Grand Opening of the store," Mother admonished. She was surrounded by boxes and cartons that were rolling in the back door of new Big Store.

Apparently, the birth of a child was not in the schedules of the busy people around me.

The transition to Big Store began after Mother, Dorcas, and I returned from the L.A. gift show. It was a good thing that we were moving into larger quarters for Little Store had reached a breaking point. Another case of mimeograph paper and the walls would crumble. Incoming product from the gift show had to go somewhere.

As fall descended, Jeff and I helped Mother and Dad trolley merchandise three doors down the street to their new location. We pushed hand trucks, wagons, and wheelbarrows piled with ledgers, carbon paper, mucilage, ring binders, and quadrille pads. We sold merchandise on the fly as customers came to town to purchase expanding files, clasp envelopes, or greeting cards. For most of a month we operated out of two locations and even from the sidewalk between.

Viktor and Dorcas joined the parade carting ink blotters, binder clips, bookkeeping systems, briefcases, and business card files from Little Store to soon-to-be-opened Big Store.

And then . . .*KRRRRASH!*

An arsenal of bullet-proof filing systems cascaded to the floor of Little Store. Dad and Dorcas had been transferring card cabinets, cash boxes, and copy holders onto a rolling cart to be moved to their new home. Viktor stood above them on a ladder handing down desk-top organizers that lined the upper shelves of the store. Viktor passed a cumbersome eight-tier horizontal file down to Dorcas. Dorcas, in turn, attempted to transfer the awkward object to the top of a teetering stack of desk trays, book racks, vertical files, and posting tubs – all of industrial weight metal. The offending file toppled, and then careened sharply toward the floor, impaling Dad's left foot as it landed. A sharp corner slashed his shoe, pierced his arch, and likely broke a toe or two. The rubble from the fall-out settled around Dad and Dorcas.

"Oh, my goodneth!" Viktor wailed. He peered wide-eyed from the top rungs of the ladder. "Do thomething, Dorcath! Do thomething!"

Dorcas urged Dad into a sitting position atop a file box. She proficiently unlaced his scuffed brogan, removed the shoe, and then peeled off a blood-saturated stocking.

"Call an ambulanth! Call an ambulanth!" Viktor clung to the upper reaches of the ladder like a paranoid monkey.

Dorcas competently looked around for something to staunch blood that was puddling on the floor. "This will have to do for now." She pulled a lace hankie that was folded neatly into her blouse pocket and plastered it over the gash, then secured the makeshift dressing with duct tape from a nearby display.

"Call an ambulanth!" Viktor repeated lamely. He remained glued to the ladder.

"Nah," Dad grunted. "I don't need an ambulance." But his voice was decidedly shaky. He sat among the dented wreckage of the avalanche weakly cradling his injured foot.

"Is this a conspiracy to do-in the owner of the stationery store?" Dad added a bit of levity to the situation.

The landslide of metal files seemed to create a bond between new owner and seasoned employees. Viktor and Dorcas had been comfortable in routines that their old jobs had provided. The transfer in owners and a move to a bigger store upset the equilibrium. Now they saw Dad as a tough but good natured employer. They threw themselves whole-heartedly into assembling New Big Store.

For the remainder of the move Dad hobbled about bearing the badge of the maimed. His foot, swathed in gauze strips, was cushioned by an old terry slipper. And ever after, a slight limp, especially when he was tired, was a reminder of the move to New Big Store.

Big Store tripled the sales space of Little Store. Viktor, now, had a full array of typewriter ribbons at his fingertips. He could provide a ribbon for any office machine on the market without making a "thpethial" order that would take a week to fill.

Dorcas, now, had four Hallmark Card racks to administer. Not only did she order Taylor Albums, but she ordered Samuels' Albums, too. And she polished the shelves of four pen cases to display fine writing instruments of great variety.

In honor of the new location Dad incorporated the business under a new name. Big block letters installed at the top of the building and fancy gold leaf painted on the front door proclaimed the opening of

Chandler Stationers
Purveyor of Office Supplies
and
Fine Gifts

17

We'll just stand at the counter and sell things.

Well, the doctor had plenty of time to see the Detroit Tigers beat the St. Louis Cardinals in the 1968 World Series.

"That baby" took a long and leisurely route into this world. But, she did hit two of the dire admonishments. She made her entrance precisely during opening day of elk season as well as the day that Mother and Dad began their grand opening celebration of New Big Store.

Chapter 5

A NEW CAREER

"What kind of businessman is Andy Akers?" I grumbled to Dad. "He charges a fifteen-cent Bic pen once a month. It's not worth using a five-cent stamp to send him a statement."

"And he doesn't think it is worth using a five-cent stamp to pay his bill," Dad replied. "Let it ride."

The first time that I encountered Andy he stepped up to the cash register and flipped a Bic on the counter. "Charge it," he smirked.

"What is your name?" I requested. Newbie that I was, I couldn't put account names and faces together.

"Howdy Doody," the man replied. Then he cackled deliriously when I started to write across the top of the invoice the name that he had given me.

Not only was Andy Akers a cheapskate, he was a comedian. His legion of Bic pens built up for months before he finally paid his bill.

I was the first person Mother and Dad hired after they bought the store. That is, apart from Viktor and Dorcas who were already on staff. I was offered a part-time job that was just right for a young mother with two little girls (one a babe in a bassinette). I would be keeper of accounts receivable.

Before the advent of VISA and MasterCard, established customers had charge accounts at our store. "Charge it," they'd say when they brought items up to the check-out counter. And their purchases would be duly recorded on charge slips that were stacked near the cash register.

A couple of times a week I retrieved the slips and took them to my improvised office to process. Hunched over a multi-tiered posting system at my kitchen table I came to know colorful people in the community of Chandler by name and business habits before I knew them by face. We had inherited an eclectic cross-section of customers from the previous stationery store owners. Diamond processors, grocery store magnates, hotel tycoons, and military officers scribbled their names or initials across invoices that we itemized. Many of our customers were connected to the agriculture industry – farm equipment sales and service, cotton gins, irrigation specialists, hay balers, crop dusters, veterinarians as well as farmers, dairymen, and ranchers.

Through the day charge request went as such:

"Put this on the Briggs Farm account." Jimmy Briggs charged a slide rule for his trigonometry class.

"Add three green Cross refills to Bashas' account." Eddie Basha, president of Bashas' Markets used only green ink for his corporate signature.

"Charge these as index cards. The office budget does not have a line item for greeting cards." A secretary in the Chandler School District offices walked out of the store with a handful of get-well cards for sick teachers.

"We'll send a man over this afternoon. Have an invoice ready." Williams Air Force Base ordered one hundred imprinted blue and gold napkins for the graduation banquet of its latest class of pilots.

The equipment I needed to process these simple charges inundated our home and totally consumed the small room that we eventually designated as an office/den.

A state-of-the-arts electronic comptometer commanded prime display space in the front window of the store. This ten-key wonder with multiple functions was on the cutting edge of office equipment. And it was for sale. Clickity-click, zip, zip. As fingers danced over the keys, a long tape peeled off a spindle and curled over the desk. A clever bookkeeper could operate the machine with his left hand as he held pen in right hand poised to record figures into a ledger.

But the comptometer was not what Dad gave me to process accounts receivable. Instead he unearthed a relic of the middle ages that operated in much the same manner as an abacus. Nine columns of keys, eight rows across, studded the top of the machine. Seventy-two keys in all – a row of ones, a row of twos, a row of threes – you get the idea. A complicated series of print bars, similar to typewriter keys popped up and down from the machine. After every entry I pulled the machine's handle and the figures that I pressed jumped onto a paper roll. The most that this machine could tabulate was $999,999.99. In our fledgling business that limitation was not a problem.

In a nod to mid-Twentieth Century, a Speed-O-Print machine alleviated the arduous work of hand-addressing statements. I called it the ker-chunk machine. At the beginning of each month I stacked little metal plates embossed with customers' names and addresses into the carriage of the machine. I carefully positioned a fresh statement over an inked ribbon, then slammed the handle down. *Ker-chunk.* The used address plate was spit into a holding tray, and the resulting statement was properly addressed for the new month's business. One by one, *ker-chunk, ker-chunk,* monthly statements rolled out, properly addressed. At this point I was ready to transcribe details from the invoices onto the statements.

A problem arose if these little metal plates got out of order or, heaven forbid, if a stack of plates spilled over the floor. They were arranged in reverse alphabetical order so that, after being stamped, the statements ended up alphabetically correct and could be easily filed with the yellow customer cards in the posting tray. If the plates spilled, not only did I have to know my alphabet backwards, I had to be able to read the mirror image of the names and addresses pressed into the plates.

Occasionally Dad asked me to report to the store to help out. Then, I packed up my tykes – bibs, bottles, and bassinette – and carted them to work with me. Infant Beth slumbered in her basket, and three-year-old Heather built forts and castles with empty boxes in the stock room.

When I was in high school I had worked in a drug store. I didn't know a depilatory from a suppository and a lot embarrassed confusion was the result. Now, I entered the world of office supplies. Beyond file folders, paper clips, and Big Chief writing tablets, I knew equally little about office supplies.

"Viktor, where are the sheet lifters?" *What in the world is a sheet lifter?*

"The theet lifterth are nexth to the note bookths." Viktor pointed me to boxes of pressboard pages that were intended to be inserted into the fronts of ring binders.

"What is a slide fastener?" "A Bulldog clip?" "A ticket holder?" "An arch file?"

"Dorcas, do we have refills for this album?" "Where is the Crane paper?" "This lady would like to have her Bible personalized."

Was there no end to the obscure things that people requested? I only wished that two people in a day would ask for the same item so that I could lead them purposefully to the object. During my early days in the store I was more a hindrance than a help to the long-suffering Viktor and Dorcas.

But I began to get a taste of what owning a store meant. In addition to demanding and sometimes quirky customers, heavy loads, tall ladders, blankets of dust, and mountains of files, the store owner's life was comprised of: long hours (six days a week, from eight in the morning until six at night); tired feet (countless miles treading up and down the aisles); short lunches (PB&J sandwiches while checking incoming orders); rules and regulations (city ordinances, OSHA regulations, fire department regulations, bank regulations, insurance regulations); and taxes, taxes, taxes (obligatory taxes to Federal, State, County, and City agencies).

Mother and Dad did not own the store. The store owned them.

Chapter 6

IT'S A SMALL WORLD

"It's like opening Christmas packages in July." I lifted a globe from its well-cushioned box and set it on the counter. With a flick of my finger I set the orb spinning. A kaleidoscope of colors, pink and green and yellow and blue, whirled before me.

I was always delighted when Dad asked me to come to the store to help check in a big order that had arrived. There was a strict protocol in checking the products received against the packing slip, pricing the items, and finding display space on the shelves. Still a novelty to me, the task helped me learn the merchandise in the store.

Dad and I had just finished unpacking an order of world globes, and now a row of spheres spun on the countertop – tabletop globes and pedestal globes. Most of them were twelve inches in diameter, good for a classroom or for a home library. A couple of antique-looking globes whose geographical boundaries were politically up-to-date nestled in carved wooden cradles. The focal object of the new display was a commanding sixteen-inch illuminated replica of the earth that retailed for $189, a definite splurge.

"Even if we don't sell this one right away it draws attention to the display," Dad said.

The new Mrs. Allenspach tottered in while the orbs were still spinning. Big Red Allenspach owned the John Deere dealership at the edge of town. A lot of tractors passed through his agency, and a lot of wives passed through his life. I had heard that this was Wife-Number-Four. We had not known Numbers One and Two. However, we were briefly acquainted with Number Three when we first moved into Little Store. Wife-Number-Three was a former Miss Cotton, a coveted title among beauties who lived in the Arizona Cotton Belt. She was still quite a beauty a couple of decades beyond her reign.

By the time we had settled into New Big Store Wife-Number-Three had been supplanted by Wife-Number-Four.

Like her predecessor, the new Mrs. Allenspach had a bushel of bleached blonde hair. Also, like her predecessor, she wore tight dresses and spiky-heeled shoes. I didn't know if the new Mrs. Allenspach held an agricultural royalty title, but she appeared to be younger than Number Three and perhaps a bit more flamboyant. At any rate, like her predecessor, she was pleasant if not a bit more scatterbrained. She was a good customer for the time being.

"Why, Mr. Harrison, what do you have here?" The new Mrs. Allenspach bestowed upon my father a "Ravish-Me-Red" smile.

"Hello, Mrs. Allenspach," Dad beamed. "We have a new display of globes."

Dad is a sucker for pretty ladies.

"Oh, what are they for?" She batted her fringed eyes.

What a ditz! Surely she knows what a globe is!

"A globe is a scale model of the earth," Dad said.

"Why, isn't that nice!" the new Mrs. Allenspach gushed.

"A globe is the only *true* map of the world because there is no distortion in the relationships of areas."

Dad is in his element. He loves to expound.

Dad put his finger on the equator of the nearest globe and spun it on its 23-degree axis. Indonesia, Papua New Guinea, the Marshall Islands, South America, and Africa spun deliriously.

"Is this the beginning of the globe?" The new Mrs. Allenspach pointed to a spot on the Indian Ocean where Dad had begun his preliminary spin.

The beginning of a globe! Get real!

"Because a world globe is round, it has no beginning or end," Dad continued.

Dad is on a roll.

"How interesting."

The new Mrs. Allenspach's eyes are glazing over.

"There are two imaginary reference lines from which all distances and locations are determined." Dad pointed out the equator and the prime meridian.

"Hmmm. . . I see."

Dad's losing her.

"We also brought in a pair of globe bookends. They might be nice in your library," Dad continued.

If the new Mrs. Allenspach has a library!

Dad had more to say. "This is a moon globe." He pointed to a gray pocked orb studded with mountains and craters. Otherworldly names like Aristarchus, Seleucus, and Ptolemaeus dotted its surface. "You can see where Apollo made its landing last year."

Surely the new Mrs. Allenspach saw that momentous event on television.

"And this is a celestial globe." Dad picked up a globe of the heavens. "You can see that it is clear. The view from Earth is from the center of this globe. Because the globe is transparent we view the stars in their proper positions *through* the globe."

Sorry, Dad, you've lost the new Mrs. Allenspach.

He picked up a dinosaur globe. "The kids should like this one. You can see where dinosaurs lived around the world millions of years ago." Dad, himself, was like a kid with this one. He pointed out ichthyosaurus, brachiosaurus, and tyrannosaurus as well as other monsters that roamed the planet from North Pole to South.

"You certainly have a big variety of globes," Mrs. Allenspach commented lamely.

We don't have any globes of Arizona.

The new Mrs. Allenspach is overwhelmed.

Dad smiled. He could feel a sale in the making.

It would be a nice perk to sell an item like a globe as soon as it comes out of the crate.

The new Mrs. Allenspach repeated, "A nice variety."

For several moments she appeared to be pondering her options. Then her eyes lit up. She seemed to realize what she wanted.

"But, Mr. Harrison, I *would* be interested in a globe of Arizona. Do you have a globe of Arizona?"

Dad's jaw dropped. World Globes, historic globes, moon globes, celestial globes, even dinosaur globes. The selection was there.

"No, ma'am," Dad shook his head wearily. "We don't have any globes of Arizona."

Chapter 7

ELROY

The first time we saw Elroy he stood in the middle of the intersection at Arizona Avenue and Williams Field Road waving merrily to north and southbound traffic as it whizzed past him. Then when the light changed, he turned and waved to east and westbound vehicles as they hurled by. This intersection was a primary crossroads before entering the business district of Chandler. The road going east terminated at Williams Air Force Base; the road going north led to Mesa.

Jeff was driving me to the store to pick up charge slips so that I could resume posting my accounts receivable.

"What is that nut doing?" Jeff growled as we skirted the improvised traffic monitor without mishap.

Elroy, we were to learn, was a fixture in downtown Chandler. Some considered him the unofficial town greeter, for not only did he hail passing vehicles, he nodded genially to pedestrians he encountered along the sidewalk often extending his hand to encourage hand-outs. A number of businessmen obliged by dropping dimes and nickels into Elroy's open palm.

He was a gimpy little guy who wore faded dungarees and oversized white T-shirts. He walked with a rolling gait favoring his right side and dragging his left foot. His bulbous nose and his bewhiskered chin met somewhere over his mouth giving him a remarkable resemblance to Popeye. Even the white cloth cap that covered his thinning hair was much like a sailor hat. The circular brim could be turned up or down; the hat could be squared, rolled, or crushed, but Elroy usually wore it like a Dixie Cup on top of his head. All that he lacked was a pipe and a can of spinach to complete the persona of the comical sailor man.

Elroy didn't seem to patronize of any of the stores on the square with the exception of Dudding's Drug Store. If he amassed enough coins during his limp around the block he went to the soda fountain and ordered a strawberry ice-cream cone, sometimes even a double-scoop treat.

"Oh, he's harmless," said Arnold who owned the Clip Joint next door. Elroy mingled with guys sitting on the bench outside the barbershop as they waited for haircuts.

"Elroy lives over at Blanche's Place. Blanche takes care of people who can't care for themselves," Arnold continued.

"It doesn't look as if she is taking care of him now," I replied. Elroy had just stepped off the curb in front of the barbershop without regard for a plumber's van rumbling down the street.

Elroy waved pleasantly to the driver who had brought the van to a screeching stop rearranging a cargo of wrenches, pipes, drains, and faucets. A toilet heading to a new construction site was upended.

"God takes care of drunks and fools," I gasped.

"That man should not be let on the streets!" Janelle Jones joined our conversation. Janelle and her daughter owned a small boutique specializing in casual fashions. "His panhandling offends the ladies coming into the shop."

I saw both sides of the coin. Elroy was disarmingly simple. But, I, like Janelle, did not like to have him panhandling in front of our store. Mostly, however, I was concerned that he would be hit by a car. His blatant disregard for traffic was legendary.

Rumor had it that Elroy was a whiz at dominoes. Some days, on his foray into town, he carried a well-worn box of double-twelves in a satchel slung over his shoulder.

On those days he wandered into Luigi's Tavern and challenged imbibers to a match. Whether the saloon patrons thought they could outdo Elroy in wits over bones and pips, or whether they liked to watch his calculator mind tally the dots and sweep up the scores, Elroy had no trouble getting takers for these penny-ante games. With his winnings, he went into Dudding's and came out licking a strawberry ice-cream cone.

Elroy's domino endeavors did not escape the watchful eyes of the pastor of the Glory Tabernacle. Brother Grant called on Elroy who throughout his life had been a devout member of the congregation.

"Playing dominoes for money is gambling," the pious preacher gently explained to Elroy. "Gambling is a sin."

Elroy took to heart the error of his ways. He packed away his box of dominoes forever.

Chapter 8

POMP AND CIRCUMSTANCE

"That is not how my name is spelled! C-H-E-R-Y-L! Not S-H-E-R-Y-L!" Cheryl Lynn Hobbs shrieked when she opened her box of name cards.

"I need fifty announcements. I have lots of relatives. There are only twenty-five in this package." Joe Sanchez complained.

"I paid for the whole order last fall. I don't owe anything!" howled Greg Mason.

Mark Bachus sidled in. "I didn't think I was going to graduate, so I didn't order announcements when the rep was at school. Since I made it, my Mom wants me to get twenty-five."

Tradition! Chandler Stationers dispensed the Chandler High School graduation announcements. But we had nothing to do with taking the orders.

In late fall a representative from Empire Engraving Company came to the Chandler High School Campus and gave his spiel to the senior class about the importance of sharing pomp and circumstance with friends and relatives. Empire, the company dominating the market on school graduation paraphernalia, was located in Denver. From their hub, graduation specialties spewed over the western region of the U.S., finely engraved announcements featuring official school crests, personalized name cards, memory books, and thank you notes.

The kids, at the height of grandeur and self-importance, filled out their graduation orders at school and gave them to the Empire representative along with a small deposit.

Time passed. And in April boxes of graduation supplies arrived at Chandler Stationers. We did this as a courtesy to the school. The school bookstore was relieved of the task of sorting through the boxes and compiling the orders. And we received a small percent of each order for our *minimal* efforts.

A master order sheet listed every student's name and the quantity of each item that he wanted – announcements, name cards, thank you notes, or memory books. The master sheet also indicated the original deposit made and the final amount due.

Our job was to sort this out. The announcements came in one giant box. Chandler High School Wolves finely engraved on heavy white vellum, along with the location (Austin Field), date (May 21, 196-), and time of the ceremony (7:00 p.m.). We carefully counted out the announcements per each student's order and placed them in smaller fold-out boxes that Empire provided. Name cards, personalized with students' names engraved on matching vellum, were pre-packaged in smaller boxes of fifty or one-hundred as the students had ordered them. We placed the name cards on top of the announcements and added assorted thank you notes or memory books depending on the order.

To each little box that measured about 6x6x8 we prepared and affixed a hand lettered invoice listing the items therein, the cost of the order, the deposit paid, and the amount due. Two hundred boxes of graduation announcements occupied significant space across our back shelves.

Year after year things went wrong. Names were misspelled. Cards didn't come. There were misunderstandings about deposits. Students changed their orders. Students didn't pick up their orders. We wanted to do right by the graduating seniors, but we were at the mercy of the master list.

"I'm sure you'll agree that this is a losing endeavor," Dorcas sagely proclaimed.

And for once Dad did agree.

We complained to Chandler High School. We complained to Empire Engraving Company.

But come fall Empire Engraving appeared at our counter again with an alternate proposal. Students would still come to our store to pick up their graduation announcements, but the orders would be fully assembled at Empire. Graduation product would arrive at our store with invoices adhered to the individual orders. We simply had to dispense the packages and collect the amount due. Any changes, disagreements, or complaints would be handled by Empire.

"You don't even have to look inside the boxes," Mr. Empire Rep assured us earnestly. "And, of course, you will be compensated for your *minimal* effort."

"That sounds easy enough," Dad said.

"Eathy peethy," mimicked Viktor.

And next April two-hundred sealed boxes containing prepackaged graduation announcements, name cards, and notes were delivered to the store. We arranged them alphabetically on the back shelves and waited for the students to file in.

All went well when Maria Chavez picked up her order. "Thanks," she said and bounced out with fifty announcements and cards that she had ordered.

And Randall Denning didn't complain when we told him his balance due was twenty-nine dollars.

Earlene Halbut's mother wished Earlene hadn't ordered so many announcements. "We don't have fifty friends and relatives to send them to." However, she took the order as presented with good grace.

But feathers hit the fan when Sam Santori stormed back in the store. And then Martha Tindall. And then Becka Williams. When these students opened their packages they found announcements, *not* to Chandler High School graduation, but to *Coleman High School* graduation!

"Whea in tham hill ith Coleman High Thkool?" shrieked Viktor.

"Coleman, *TEXAS?*" Dorcas's inflection went up a decibel as she read the details of the announcement.

I pulled a Hammond's Atlas off the shelves. Coleman, Texas was a spot on the road south of Abilene. Another CHS with the same royal blue class color as Chandler High School had selected a very similar graduation announcement style.

We got out the old box cutters, and beginning with Edward Adams we opened the boxes of announcements that remained on the shelves. To our dismay every student whose last name began with the letter R through the end of the alphabet had received the erroneous Coleman High School announcements! Empire had co-mingled the school graduation announcements.

Empire made good on their error. They stopped the presses and made a special and generous run of Chandler High School graduation announcements. By the next week a crate of corrected cards came through our door via special delivery. And, as in previous years, our *minimal* effort included carefully counting the announcements and repackaging the incorrect parcels.

Chapter 9

CHECK YOUR GUN AT THE DOOR

"Futht I have to twain the new ownerth in how to wun an offith thupply thtore." Viktor was overheard complaining to Maybelle, Dr. Blanding's office manager.

"Then, I get them moved to thith new locathon," he continued. "And now they bwing in thome young buck fwom the mountainth who hath to check hith gun at the door."

But, I digress.

* * *

Three years had passed since the stationery store in Chandler had moved into its larger quarters. With the move down the street, larger space, and greater inventory, business at Chandler Stationers was actually growing. What could be better than one stationery store? Two stationery stores!

"Quantity buying," said Dad. "That's the only way to get ahead in this business."

It so happened that just as Dad and Mother were getting the hang of being merchants, a store very similar to Chandler Stationers came up for sale in central Phoenix. Like Chandler Stationers, this business had been operating since the 1930s. Age and health concerns were forcing the long-time owners to step down. *Déjà vu.*

Indian School Stationers was located on a major artery of Phoenix, Indian School Road. The road (and later the store) was so named because Phoenix Indian School was an historic landmark on that route. The BIA boarding school was established in 1891 for Indian students in grades one through twelve. By this time in its history PIS was a high school serving students from tribes across the nation. The school, located seven blocks from its store namesake, was an established customer of the store.

"I will buy that store," declared Dad. "It is well-located. It has an established customer base. With two stores I will have greater purchasing power."

"It will also put us closer to home," Mother agreed.

The commute to Chandler from their home in northwest Phoenix was beginning to take a toll on Mother. A sixty-mile-round-trip across the girth of Phoenix added almost an hour to each end of a long work day. If Mother set up shop at Indian School Stationers she would be a mere five miles from home.

With a second store under his belt Dad began ordering paper by the pallet, ring binders by the gross, and chalk boards by the dozens. Product was divided between the two stores. Dad shuffled daily between Phoenix and Chandler, his little Datsun pickup groaning under file cabinets, storage boxes, and catalog racks being transferred one direction or the other. Mother settled herself into an office at Indian School Stationers (henceforth dubbed I.S.). From that dais she ruled over payroll and accounts payable for both stores. She seldom ventured across town to see what the appendage in Chandler was doing.

And I was called to pinch-hit more and more frequently in Chandler.

"I really need a full-time manager in Chandler," Dad said to me one day as he plopped a final case of duplicator paper at Chandler's back door. "I don't spend enough time here to keep things on track."

I had always thought my wiry bantam rooster of a dad was indefatigable, his energy unflagging. On this day he actually looked weary.

"What about Viktor?" I ventured. After all, Viktor came with the inventory in Chandler. He, of all people, knew the product in the store.

"Bah," said Dad. "If Viktor had anything on the ball, he would own this store by now!"

Viktor was stingy. "Mithter Hawwithon," Viktor shook his head dismally, "thath a mighty big order of tape dithpentherth. "We have thixth on the thelveth already."

Viktor was not adaptable. "Mithter Hawwithon, I don't mean to complain, but we have alwayth put thithers nextht to thtaplerth."

Viktor was a tattletale. "Mithter Hawwithon, I'm thure it wath a mithtake, but Thuthan forgot to add a penthil tharpener to Mithus Theagalth order."

Viktor did have his redeeming qualities. Nobody knew typewriter ribbons like Viktor. Nu-Kote ribbons, sequentially numbered from 1-100, fit every typewriter and adding machine on the market. Adler, Allen, Brother, Clary, Corona, Olivetti, Remington, Royal. Without referring to the cross reference chart hanging at the end of the counter Viktor could lay his hands on precisely the ribbon Mrs. Dixon needed for her Underwood 150FS. For that alone it was worth keeping Viktor around. But as manager material . . .

"I was thinking about Jeff," said Dad.

* * *

Wow, Jeff! My sinewy groom of ten years didn't seem like a store manager to me. He was a wildlife manager. (By this I mean the manager of wild animals, not wild night-life.) For two years during his graduate school days he trooped around the mountains in the Mohave Desert observing bighorn sheep for his master's thesis. For eight years he had been employed by the Arizona Game and Fish Department as a research biologist studying habits of deer on the Four Peaks Mountains. He collected javelina stomach samples at hunter check stations, tracked mountain lions, and monitored the buffalo hunt. Occasionally he trailed wildlife from the vantage point of a helicopter. And once he delivered a blind elk to the wildlife veterinary school in Fort Collins for research.

Jeff loved his job. But it took its toll on our family. He was away most of the time. When Jeff was out in the field he was in his element. But periodically he was assigned to the Phoenix office to prepare reports of all the statistics he had scribbled in his field journals. Formalizing reports was his nemesis. Writing a final report ranked right along with getting a root canal.

* * *

"No way!"

"It's something to think about."

"I don't know any more about merchandising than I do about tap dancing."

"Neither did Mother or Dad."

"Yeah, your dad has guts, gumption, and gusto. Who would have believed a road builder would end up selling Rolodexes."

"By the way, you did a great job setting up that Rolodex display."

"A simple matter of fitting peg A into slot A and tightening the screw. That doesn't make me an expert on Rolodexes!" Jeff grabbed a piece of cold toast and smeared it with marmalade.

"And your mother doesn't even like me," he snarled.

"She didn't like any of my boyfriends," I contended. "But you're growing on her."

This heated conversation took place over breakfast one fall morning. Jeff took a swig of tepid coffee and grimaced. Sticky remnants of fried egg (over easy) rimmed his plate.

"G'bye, Mom." Six-year-old Heather dashed in and planted a kiss on my cheek. "G'bye, Daddy. When will you be home?"

"I'll be back Friday, Munchkin." Jeff hugged his older child. "Take care of Mommy for me."

The door slammed and Heather darted to the corner school bus stop.

"*That* Baby" Beth, whose birth had thrown a kink in

the elk hunt, was now a three-year-old. She wandered into the back yard to play in the sandbox.

I stretched and arched my aching back. Tepid coffee, runny eggs. I gagged. Any day now I would bring another child into the fold. Hopefully not before Friday. Fortunately, Jeff did not have a hunting permit competing with the birth of his third child.

Check your gun at the door.

* * *

Whatever transpired between Dad and Jeff was challenging, convincing, and compensatory, to boot. Not that it required an immediate decision on Jeff's part. He considered his options. Perhaps his decision was weighted when our newborn had minor surgery on her ears and Jeff wanted to be with us at the time.

He summed it up succinctly after agreeing to take the job.

"Well, if I can load a hunting gun, I guess I can load a staple gun."

Chapter 10

HUNTING SEASON

Jeff dropped the badge that identified him as a deputized game ranger into a catch-all box harboring wine corks, screws, fuses, never-used tie clips, and miscellaneous keys to unknown locks. He doffed the khaki uniform shirt of Game and Fish and donned a new uniform of pressed chinos and button-down shirts. He looked downright dapper setting off to work, lunchbox in hand. Now Jeff shuttled merchandise back and forth across metropolitan Phoenix in a little Datsun pickup. Instead of a gun rack in the back window, a catalog rack was in the front seat.

* * *

Andy Akers owned an insurance agency on the north side of the plaza. He got on Dad's bad side early on when he came into the store hawking his insurance plans.

"Three years running I was top Benefit Life Salesman in the district," Andy boasted as he scribbled his name across the bottom of a charge slip. In addition to his monthly Bic pen Andy had magnanimously added a box of file folders to his order.

"You don't say," muttered Dad.

"Old Red Allenspach has all his insurance policies with Akers insurance. Fact is Red just took out a hundred-thou life insurance policy on that new wife of his."

"I won't buy insurance from a man who can't keep his mouth shut," Dad grumbled as Andy went out the door.

* * *

Jeff had recently stepped in as manager of Chandler Stationers. He was testing the waters and was gradually becoming acquainted with the clientele. He had yet to meet Andy Akers.

One day a man stepped up to the cash register, pen in hand. "Put this on my bill, Sonny. Name's Andy Akers." He flipped a Bic onto the counter under the startled nose of the new store manager.

Jeff quietly assessed the visage before him. Flushed face and glassy eyes, suggestive of a man who ends each day with a toddy or two. Good haircut, graying hair parted sharply then combed carefully over a receding brow line. Blue striped necktie encircling the collar of a starched white shirt. Soft in the paunch, his belt secured gabardine pants around his portly girth.

"One. Bic. Pen." Jeff spoke each word deliberately. He cocked an eyebrow as he retrieved a charge slip from the drawer.

"I need to order a rubber stamp, too," the man identified as Andy Akers continued.

Jeff procured the rubber stamp catalog from the drawer and opened it to a page displaying type styles available for custom-made stamps.

Andy Akers poured over fonts and the sizes. He seemed to be comparing the display to a sample he held in his hand.

"This'll do." He settled on a line of narrow Arial type and told Jeff to have the following crafted into a rubber stamp.

ANTELOPE
Unit 12
October 27-31, 197_

Computers had not taken over the business world, nor had they taken over the world of the Arizona Game and Fish

Department. Just as today, hunters applied for big-game hunts (e.g. elk, deer, antelope, turkey) months before the seasons were underway. Applications were tossed into a revolving cage then physically extracted one by one. Successful draws were validated by rubber stamp with the name of the hunt, the geographical unit in the state for which they were drawn, and the dates of that hunt. Properly drawn and validated applications were sent back to jubilant hunters along with tags to tie around the quarries' legs. All the other applications were returned to the hunters with UNSUCCESSFUL stamped across the page and refunds enclosed.

Drawing for a big-game hunt was a labor intensive process. Extensive lists were compiled. Arizona Game and Fish knew exactly who was entitled to hunt in each of its regions. Those lists were sent to game managers in districts throughout the state. During hunting season check stations were posted at each of the units, and hunters were supposed to stop and show their validated hunt permits.

Most hunters are true sportsmen. They hunt in season and abide by the rules. They throw their hunting applications into the lottery and rejoice when they are drawn. The outdoor experience and camping camaraderie is as important as the hunt. Nevertheless, the system at that time allowed ample opportunity for nefarious hunters to slip through the cracks.

Until now, Jeff had not known Andy Akers. And Andy Akers did not know the new manager of Chandler Stationers. More importantly, Andy did not know that the new manager had, until recently, worked for Arizona Game and Fish. In fact, Jeff had worked on many of the hunt drawings.

Jeff could see immediately what this dude was up to. He was *not* going to submit an application for the antelope hunt. He would not subject himself to the one-in-twenty chance of being drawn for the coveted hunt. Instead, he would pick up a hunt application form at the Yellow Front Store, fill it out, and with a custom-made rubber stamp would stamp ANTELOPE, Unit 12 across the application. He had selected a rubber stamp font remarkably like the stamps AG&F used. Voila! A validated permit! He would skirt the required check station to avoid having his "permit" checked against the master list of valid hunters. If, by chance, he ran into a game warden in the field during antelope season, he would flash his improperly stamped application and be on his way. Only the most discerning of game wardens would see the difference. Here was that one-in-a-hundred hunter who called himself a sportsman.

Andy Akers told Jeff to add the rubber stamp to his account and left the store with a self-satisfied smirk across his face.

How often had Andy pulled this stunt? Things might be different this year. The new manager of Chandler Stationers put in a call to his pals at AG&F. The hunters for antelope in Unit 12 would be going through an extra level of scrutiny this fall.

Chapter 11

WON'T YOU, JEFF?

The apparition stopped before entering the store. Chin up, shoulders back, hands on hips, feet apart and firmly planted in the doorway. The activities of the store ground to a halt as customers and employees became aware of his presence. Dorcas's dust rag paused in mid-air as she reached to clean a what-not shelf. Mrs. Miller dropped a box of paper clips and they scattered over the floor. Clive Johnson looked up from a book he was perusing to view the situation as it unfolded.

"Koh-i-noor," the specter grunted.

He might have stepped from the pages of *Wild West Magazine*. Bronze skin, chiseled cheekbones, long black hair tamed by a red bandana tied over his left ear. He was dressed in denim dungarees laundered to a soft blue hue. His shirt, open to the navel, displayed a smooth muscular chest. High-top moccasins ended in a supple fringe below the knees. A bear-claw necklace hung around his neck. And strapped to his waist was a sheath from which protruded a bone-handled knife. Even lacking war paint, he was the epitome of a fierce savage.

"Koh-i-noor," he repeated as he strode to the front counter. This might have been interpreted as a war chant uttered before a scalping raid.

Viktor, replenishing typewriter ribbons, blanched when the fierce gaze fell upon him. He dropped what he was doing and bustled to find Jeff in the office.

"Th-Th-Thammy Thithto ith out of jail!" Viktor wheezed breathlessly, and then reached in his pocket for his inhaler. Squeeze, gasp. Squeeze, gasp. "We'll have to help him with what he needths and get him out of the thtore fatht."

"Won't you, Jeff?"

Sammy Sixto was more bluster than brute. He had spent a couple of years in prison for maiming a man in a barroom brawl. And he took advantage of his frightful demeanor to terrorize the gentry. He needed a Koh-I-Noor technical pen for his home-based drafting enterprise.

From the ridiculous to the sublime, when something had to be done that no one else wanted to do Jeff was on call.

* * *

"Signet Corporation needs a gross of the three-inch red view binders by Friday." Dad was on the telephone calling from the I.S. store.

"Wow! That's tomorrow," replied Jeff. It was Thursday, closing time.

"I told them we would deliver tomorrow afternoon – by 5:00. How many do you have in Chandler, Jeff?"

Jeff checked the shelves. "Only one three-inch red binder."

"We have a couple here," Dad added.

Three binders. That was a far cry from the 144 binders that the company wanted.

"Unified Office Products does not have those binders in stock and cannot get them from the manufacturer until next week".

Signet Corporation had probably called every office supply store in Phoenix and received discouraging information that 144 of these odd-ball binders could not be procured overnight.

"How will we fill the order?" Jeff scratched his head overcome by the futility of the deal.

Silly question. *You bet, we'll do that* was the motto of

this operation.

It carried over from the days Dad owned a gas station: *You bet, we'll service the fleet as it passes through Flagstaff.* A motorcade was travelling Route 66 from Chicago to L.A. at the end of the Great Depression.

It carried over from the days he owned a chicken ranch: *You bet, we'll have the chickens ready for market tomorrow.* The bottom fell out of the poultry market and his buyer could not pick up the flock designated for market. Dad committed to cleaning and plucking 500 pullets for grocery stores and restaurants in the Phoenix metropolis.

It carried over from the days he owned a construction company: *You bet, we'll complete that stretch of road by May 1st.* Dad went up against major contractors in the state and won a bid for a section of Interstate 17 that was on the drawing board to link Phoenix and Flagstaff.

Say you'll do it. Do it!

Procuring a gross of red view binders was small potatoes compared to some of the things Dad had done.

"Robert's Manufacturing is in the City of Industry," Dad continued. He had already done his research. "They will have twelve cases of red binders on their dock by 8:00 tomorrow morning. We'll pick them up at that time . . .

"Won't you, Jeff?"

City of Industry, California was a suburb of Los Angeles poised near to California's main freeway system. Several of our suppliers were located in this manufacturing hub. A drive to City of Industry from our home in Arizona would take seven or eight hours negotiating unfamiliar California byways.

"Guess where I'm going tonight?" Jeff dragged in after a long day's work. He ate a quick dinner, filled a thermos with hot coffee, and pulled the little Datsun around to the corner Chevron Station to fill the gas tank and check the tires. He set off on a marathon excursion He might even get a couple of hours' sleep in the cab of his truck as he waited for the warehouse to come to life.

* * *

Western Auto, an independently owned hardware store, was next door to us on the south. That was the place to buy shovels and rakes, pressure cookers and canning jars, rye seed and pruning shears, a can of paint and caulking compound. Western Auto had a little bit of anything you needed to keep hearth and home ship-shape. In the few years that we had been located in our expanded location we noticed that the inventory at Western Auto was dwindling. And then the sign went up: *Going Out of Business.* So sad. Western Auto was crumbling under the pressures of Home Improvement Capitals sprouting up in the Phoenix region and its environs.

"I'm going to look into expanding into Western Auto," Dad mused when it became evident that Western Auto's doors would be padlocked at the end of the month.

Western Auto and Chandler Stationers shared the same landlord and the same roof. They were actually two divisions of the same building. Expanding into Western Auto would double our size again.

"We could move the office products into the south side, the Western Auto side, and expand that inventory," Dad continued. "On the north side we could bring in more greeting card racks and increase the gift line."

"That would more than double our stockroom storage also," Jeff remarked. "Western Auto has an attic over their half of the building."

"We know that Owensby will agree. He just wants to keep the building leased." Dad was referring to our absentee property manager. "I'll call him today."

As Western Auto was selling their last garden hose and wheelbarrow, their last hammer and bucket of ten-penny nails, their last crock pot and toaster, Dad and Jeff were tapping the wall that separated our stores.

"The major supports for this wall are located here and

here." Dad paced off the distance between the studs. "We'll open the wall between these beams . . .

"Won't you, Jeff?"

It was *business as usual* during the renovation. Jeff changed from his chinos and button-down shirts to bib overalls with drills, mallets, and crowbars dangling from loops and pockets. For an entire summer he worked behind plastic sheeting that minimally protected merchandise and customers from the fallout of construction.

* * *

The sheriff strode through the front door. He wore pointy-toed boots, leather chaps, and a ten-gallon Stetson. But what really identified him as a man of the law was the shiny star pinned on the left side of his vest. Two grim deputies, similarly attired, followed in lock-step. They bore lassos and handcuffs.

I stood transfixed behind the cash register.

Viktor stopped mid-count in an order he was assembling for City Hall.

Dorcas looked up from the card rack she was stocking with a new shipment of spring greetings.

"Jeff McMichael!" The sheriff barked.

My husband peered from behind a rack of quadrille pads.

"In the name of the law, you are under arrest." The sheriff unfurled a document two feet in length and began to read a litany of charges. "Civil disobedience . . . disorderly conduct . . . failure to adhere to local ordinances . . ."

And he continued. "You are known to park your disreputable Datsun on a city street . . . Your employees complain that you subject them to eight-hour work days . . . We have heard that you took a football from a child who threw it in your store . . ."

The deputies stepped forward and manacled Jeff's hands behind his back.

"You have the right to remain silent . . . Anything you say or do may be used against you . . ."

To assure that their culprit did not attempt escape, the deputies looped a lasso around Jeff's shoulders and firmly directed him toward the door and to a paneled van waiting at the curb.

Jeff yowled as he was led away. "Let me explain!"

"Wha . . .whath's happening," stammered Viktor.

"I'm sure you'll agree they had good reason to be here," commented Dorcas. She turned back to her task of restocking greeting cards.

I giggled mirthfully.

Jeff was one of the businessmen caught up in the local Rotary Club's Jail and Bail Day, a fund raiser for their exchange student program.

"I suppose someone will have to post bail," I called after him.

"Won't you, Jeff?"

Chapter 12

LUIGI'S

Now that we were expanding into Western Auto's space, our immediate neighbor to the south was Luigi's. Luigi's Tavern was the ecumenical watering hole for the community. Farmers, ranchers, attorneys, insurance salesmen, and business owners stopped by Luigi's for a swill before heading home from work. Pima Indians from the reservation hobnobbed with physicians, and Mexican field hands rubbed elbows with city council members down the long scarred bar. Political shenanigans were concocted and business deals sketched out on cocktail napkins in dark booths lining the back wall.

Luigi's was a guy's place. What went on in Luigi's was an enigma to most of the women in town, at least the *nice* women in town. Occasionally we witnessed an overblown floozy entering the establishment on the arm of a sugar daddy. But most ladies scurried past the swinging doors and held their breaths against the stench of stale beer, stale smoke, and stale body odor that wafted across the sidewalk.

"Jeff, will you go into Luigi's and get Daniel for me? I need to get home." Mrs. Strathmore, wife of the distinguished senator from District 18 did not want to venture into the den of iniquity. Her husband had stepped into Luigi's for a quick quaff while she shopped. He had not come out in a timely manner.

It seemed like Luigi's was open all the time, but we

knew that, by law, they had to lock their doors between 1:00 and 6:00 a.m. By the time we opened at 8:00 in the morning, activity at Luigi's was already underway. Music tinkled behind Luigi's doors as they swung in and out for morning imbibers. As the day progressed Luigi's doors swung wider and more frequently and the music became louder.

Luigi, himself, ruled the tavern from behind the counter serving as bartender as well as bouncer. Not often did I actually see the guy, a great mountain of a man who reminded me of Bluto in the old Popeye comic strip. He had a small head, thick neck, and a perpetual five o'clock shadow that stretched from ear to ear across his face. I certainly would not have wanted to cross him.

Evenings were lively at Luigi's, particularly Friday evenings. Friday was pay day on many of the ranches, so a crowd with money jingling in their pockets convened at the tank. On Saturday mornings we occasionally found blood on the sidewalk suggesting that a brawl had occurred as Luigi rousted out the imbibers who were reluctant to leave his establishment at closing time.

During the period that Jeff was expanding and remodeling the store he was installing shelves along the south wall, the wall that abutted Luigi's.

"Bzzzza- bzzzza-bzzzza," went his saw.

"Whrrrr-whrrrr-whrrrr," went his drill.

"Wham-bang-bang," went his hammer.

Luigi lumbered through our door. "What'sa goin' on?" he yelled. In spite of his dish towel and white apron he looked pretty fierce.

"You're knocking down my bottles of booze!"

Luigi had spent the afternoon catching liters of Johnny Walker, Jim Beam, and Jack Daniels as they shimmied to the edges of his shelves.

But all was tit for tat. After we settled into the newly refurbished south half of the store we received a call in the wee hours of the morning.

"This is the Chandler Police Department."

"Your burglar alarm is shrieking," a dispatcher continued. "Someone will have to come to the store to turn off the alarm and check things out. An officer will meet you there."

A call like that pretty much shot the night. Jeff dragged out of bed, pulled his pants over his pajamas and stuck his sockless feet into sheepskin lined mocs. A ten mile stretch between our home and the store was before him. Fortunately, at 1:30 in the morning, traffic was light. Once he passed the street lights of Mesa, a dark two-lane route between fields of cotton and alfalfa led to Chandler.

Closing time at Luigi's could be a rowdy affair. In the kerfuffle, unruly inebriates had knocked against our windows setting off our burglar alarm. The topers scattered, leaving behind an empty street and an ear-piercing squall that punctuated the night air.

Faint pink hues lined the eastern horizon when Jeff slipped back into bed. He optimistically hoped for another hour of sleep.

"I'm going to employ a jack hammer when I light into the south wall of the stockroom," he muttered before drifting off.

I believe Jeff had visions of Johnny Walker, Jim Beam, and Jack Daniels again dancing off the shelves.

Chapter 13

THE ATTIC

When I was a child I lost myself in the lavishly illustrated *One Thousand and One Nights*. Prominent in those Arabian tales was the flying carpet, a transportation device that carried passengers from place to place in the twinkling of an eye. The magic carpet of legend was woven of silk threads laced with gold. It unfurled to transport Ali or Sinbad across a star-studded sky to a secret lair full of incalculable riches.

Chandler Stationers had its own magical transport that carried the venturesome to an obscure labyrinth. Tucked into an inconspicuous corner beyond the back delivery door of the store, a crude version of a flying carpet lay poised for flight. Tacked over an elevator platform five feet square, worn through to the boards in numerous spots, stained with oil and grime of the ages, our carpet was not obvious to the naked eye, for it was usually piled with boxes going to or coming from The Attic.

I speak of The Attic with hushed reverence. To most of our employees The Attic was a place of untold mystery. Product would disappear into The Attic only to reappear seasonally or when needed. The only means of reaching The Attic was via the magic carpet. And few were initiated into the select brotherhood of flying carpet engineers – Jeff, a string of dare-devil stock boys, and I.

The Attic had an intriguing and patriotic history long before we came on the scene. World War II was in full swing, and Chandler was awash with Army Air Corps personnel. Nearby Williams Field was a primary training ground for twin-engine pilots headed for the European and Pacific Theaters of War. In addition to fleets of pilots stepping into the community, numerous civilians were pulled into critical jobs at the base – construction jobs, office jobs, service jobs. Williams Field could not provide housing for the vast influx of military and civilian workforce. Every available rooming house, motor lodge, and apartment in the small community of Chandler, population 1,200, was occupied. Living quarters were scabbed into all available nooks and crannies in the town.

At that time our building was occupied by an electrical contractor who supplied electrical needs about town. The front part of the store was a shop full of lamps, lighting fixtures, and small electrical appliances. Above the shop was a musty dusty attic.

Stepping up to the cry for sleeping quarters, the contractor set out to make The Attic habitable. He installed a rudimentary bathroom in the front corner – a toilet, a sink, and a shower – and he wired in electric lights that dangled from the rafters. Several cots and second-hand bureaus completed the amenities. The uninsulated boudoir was undoubtedly like an oven when temperatures rose to 115° in Arizona summers. The only air conditioning available came through open windows that overlooked the roof of the tavern next door. This odd-ball living arrangement was but one example of inconvenience and discomfort people endured during that Great War.

To provide his tenants transport to The Attic the contractor jerry-rigged an elevator. A construction worker who rented a pallet in the garret could not be faint of heart. An illegitimate union between a winch and a guillotine, the contrivance to The Attic groaned and lurched, rising slowly and dropping spasmodically. When the War was over, the need for auxiliary housing was over, too. The Attic reverted to occupancy by spiders and crickets. But then it had an elevator.

Subsequent businesses in this building made use of the elevator and the space above the store for storage. Western Auto who vacated the premise prior to our moving in had carried pails and washtubs, shovels and rakes to The Attic.

And we followed suit, moving back stock, overstock, and seasonal merchandise to The Attic. Each time I mounted the wobbly levitation machine I marveled at its history.

The elevator aka the Flying Carpet was an open-sided affair. No little scissor cage contained the rider. No rails, bars, or ropes outlined the precipitous edge. Once he began a precarious rise, the rider was hostage to the mechanism.

The machine was put into operation when a heavy rope hanging from an overhead engine hoist was pulled. The elevator growled and began an arthritic rise to the floor above. The rider had to hold the rope taut for the duration of the trip or he would be caught midway between floors.

A greasy loop of cable worked its way around overhead pulleys and dangled loosely over the center of the pallet. Seasoned conductors of the Flying Carpet sported shirts with black oily stripes across their shoulders.

Usually one riding the Flying Carpet was accompanied by a mountain of boxes traveling up to The Attic or down to the sales floor. The oddly distributed weight of the cargo caused the platform to lurch unsteadily. The engineer made a cockeyed ascent (or descent) hoping his cargo wouldn't plummet from the lift to the cement floor ten feet below.

As seasons passed we moved the accoutrements of Valentine's Day, Easter, Halloween, Thanksgiving, and Christmas up and down from The Attic via the Flying Carpet as well as storage boxes, metal files, and chalk boards – merchandise that would take no hurt from residing in the heat and dust of the garret.

The Attic became the repository of all things that had nowhere else to go. Detritus from construction ended up in The Attic – tools, lumber, electric cables, shelf brackets, floor tiles, and paint cans. An impenetrable maze of wire display racks jammed in a back corner mated and reproduced faster than coat hangers. If we sought a rack to exhibit new merchandise that came into the store, retrieving one from the wire jungle was like unlocking a giant Chinese ring puzzle.

Lacking adequate storage space in our own house, Jeff and I took advantage of the space available above the store. No need to throw it away. Store it in The Attic. A tower of foot lockers and leather trunks contained prom dresses lovingly folded away, high school year books, and college texts – *Economics ca 1959, English Literature from Beowulf to Sheridan* – no telling when I might need those again. There were things that we had a glimmer of hope of restoring – broken lamps, picture frames, tables, and chairs. And things we were not ready to give away – a crib, a playpen, a rocking horse.

Jeff added his own unique stamp to the appurtenances of The Attic – a rack of elk antlers from which hung a hunting coat, a smashed Stetson, and coils of sisal lashing; a box of coyote traps; a WWII pup tent; Coleman stoves and lanterns; a guitar with no strings, as well as questionable parts of a defunct International Travel-all – four wheels, a back seat, and a fender.

The Attic was hot, stuffy, dirty, and dim. Generally, a trip to The Attic was conducted as quickly as possible. A string of forty-watt light bulbs dangled from the center rafters casting eerie orange arcs of light. Three grimy windows overlooked the peeling rooftop tarpaper of Luigi's.

For our entire tenure in the store the only way to reach The Attic had been via the Flying Carpet.

One afternoon six burly firemen trooped into the store to conduct their annual fire inspection. A litany of violations included:

"Boxes are stacked too close to the ceiling along the south wall."

"Exit doors should be clearly labeled."

"Helium tank must be securely chained to the wall."

These breaches were easy enough to correct. But the final citation involved some time and expense.

"Stairs must be constructed to the attic to provide alternate egress."

For over forty-five years the flying carpet had gone unnoticed or at least unremarked upon by the gurus of public safety. Now we were being called to task.

Old "Clem" Clements did the job for us. He used clean new pine to create stairs and a banister to the musty dusty attic.

In spite of the edict administered by our civil servants, the flying carpet remained our primary mode of travel to The Attic. After all, using the elevator to transport mountains of boxes was much easier than carting them individually up and down the stairs. However, now the hoi polloi could ascend to The Attic without fear of plunging to their deaths.

An aura of mystery and adventure about the store was forever gone.

Chapter 14

MAKE A COPY, PLEASE

Ebenezer Scrooge employed Bob Cratchit to laboriously copy the records of his counting house. Cratchit hunched in dismal light over a slanted table. With dip pen and mulberry ink, he took great care to avoid splatting ink drops over his carefully scribed figures.

Through the years office workers have needed to make more than one copy of a document. Duplicating the written word has evolved from simple woodblocks of yesteryear to laser printers and high-speed scanners of today. Manuscripts have gone through processes such as etching, lithography, typesetting, offset printing, screen printing, and thermal printing. There was the printing press associated with the famous Gutenberg Bible. There was the polygraph, an ingenious letter copying device used by Thomas Jefferson. And there was the rotary press that allowed mass production of a page in a single day.

Chandler Stationers was mid-stream in the evolution of copying technology. We sold boxes of carbon paper. A secretary slipped a sheet of typewriter carbon behind two sheets of blank paper. A second and exact copy of the text she was typing peeled out of the machine along with the original. If the secretary needed to make multiple copies of a document, carbon sets were available. Preassembled packs of manifold paper (second and even third sheets of tissue-like paper) were interleaved with carbon for copies of correspondence and general office work.

Churches printed their weekly bulletins on Gestetner mimeograph machines. And teachers ran their tests on spirit duplicators also know as ditto machines. For these processes we provided stencils and ink.

I used the Post-Rite system of bookkeeping, a multi-tiered method of keeping accounts payable and accounts receivable. A white ledger sheet, carbon, a yellow customer account card, carbon, a white statement. Exact copies of my figures were transcribed through all layers. I posted daily into this system with a ballpoint pen, and by the end of the month a completed statement was ready to be mailed to the customer.

One summer day a fast-talking salesman came in bearing a battered briefcase. He wore a plaid sports coat over a rumpled white shirt. "Never trust a salesman who wears a coat and tie after May 1st in Arizona," Jeff grumbled. Nevertheless, he took a moment to listen to the man.

"Copy machines are the wave of the future," Mr. Plaid Coat proclaimed. He pulled from his magic bag a glossy picture of a leviathan that would occupy twenty-five square feet of precious store space.

"This is an electrostatic copying machine." He spoke reverently. "This amazing machine will produce up to ten dry-contrast copies per minute. Put one in your store and secretaries will line up to have documents reproduced. You charge ten-cents a page for the service. In addition the machine is available to you for your own duplicating needs."

Jeff scratched his chin. "By gol," he muttered.

This was a rental deal, and we were to pay the copying machine company a rather hefty sum for the privilege of using their machine. It required toners, toner intensifiers, carriers, and special rolls of paper.

Jeff was one for looking ahead, so the gargantuan contraption was installed at the back of the store near the office. And we waited for the secretaries to line up.

The machine flummoxed us. The "easy-to-load" cartridges were an enigma. We were thwarted by paper jams, and we never seemed to get the toners and the intensifiers in proper balance. This wave of the future certainly was more bother than it was worth for our purposes, and the occasional customer who asked us to copy a document usually did not accept the copy because of its anemic appearance. The electrostatic copier gathered dust at the back of the store until we called the company to take it back.

In time we got a new-fangled Xerox machine. It came with a service agreement, and at regular intervals a representative from the company came in the door with a suitcase full of tools. He spread a drop cloth around the machine, unhinged its doors, and did some tinkering with the innards of the machine. He replaced the toner and left us with cases of Xerox paper. By now the secretaries were lining up at the copier, as well as students, Sunday school teachers, and insurance agents. The public had caught on to the convenience of making copies of their projects.

* * *

Little Donny Greenlee was six years old. His grandparents owned a craft and needlework shop on the square. Martha Mimms gave needlepoint and tatting lessons to augment the stitchery kits that she sold. Stewart Mimms gave carving lessons at the back of the shop and sold fine knives and Xacto sets for the intricate craft he espoused. Often on a Saturday little Donny spent the day with Gramma and Grampa Mimms.

Time hung heavy on Donny's hands, especially when Gramma and Grampa were tied up with customers or giving lessons. We'd see Donny walking up and down the block pressing his little freckled nose against plate glass windows. He drifted in and out of the businesses. The guys sitting on the bench in front of the barber shop joshed with Donny a bit. The bootery was intriguing to the little guy because a line of saddles in the front window invited him to hop astride. However, little Donny by-passed other businesses. The tavern was off-limits. He didn't give the dress shop and the jewelry store second glances.

Of all the stores on the west side of the square the stationery store held the greatest allure for a six-year-old. Beside the cash register we had an island of colorful jee-jaws that provided Donny with a creative selection of art material. Pens, pencils, markers of every imaginable kind and color screamed, "Try me! Try me!" on pads of scratch paper. There were tubs of novelty erasers, bins of kitschy pencil sharpeners, fluorescent rulers, chalk, crayons, and glue.

One day Little Donny had a crisp dollar bill in his hand. "Grampa gave me a dollar," he said. Donny began to peruse the novelty island to determine how he could spend his money. After much deliberation he set a pile of items on the counter and presented his dollar.

"Oh, Donny," Jeff said. "You don't have enough money for all these things. You'll have to choose just one."

Little Donny's lower lip protruded petulantly. "I'll have to think," he said and collected his hoard to return the items to the shelf.

I have enough money to buy all of this stuff.

At that moment the solution to Little Donny's cash shortage presented itself. Kevin Jones had just walked away from the Xerox machine with a stack of twenty lost-dog notices he was going to post around his neighborhood. Little Donny stepped over to the machine and placed his dollar bill in the middle of the scanner as he had seen Kevin do. With the press of a button, out rolled twenty one-dollar bills, more than enough for the stash of trinkets Donny wished to purchase.

* * *

Another fast-talking salesman presented us with yet another wave of the future. "A facsimile machine," he declared. "It's called a fax. With this amazing machine you can send written documents over telephone lines. A page can be transmitted to Paris, Texas or to Paris, France in six minutes."

We brought an auxiliary phone line into the store to which a fax machine was hooked. The forty-six pound apparatus looked like a cross between a telephone and a typewriter. To operate the fax machine we simply placed a sheet of paper face down in a slot. We dialed the telephone number to which the document was being sent, pressed a button, and rollers carried the paper through a mysterious channel that captured the written word. What spit out at the receiving end was a curl of thermal paper containing a reproduction of the original piece. For the price of a telephone call, business documents flew around the world.

* * *

Paul Grub was a potato broker. Every summer he left his tuber farm in Colorado and drove to Chandler where potatoes were ready for harvest. He booked a room at the Roadrunner Lodge and made the rounds to farms surrounding Chandler. Paul spent six weeks wheeling-dealing potatoes under the name of his company, PG Potato Marketing. This enterprise involved much correspondence aimed at initiating bids, getting the best prices for the crops, and arranging for freight to supermarket chains and potato chip factories.

The new-fangled fax machine was a boon to his enterprise. No longer did Paul have to spend hours on a pay phone negotiating deals. No longer did he frequent Western Union to send telegrams out to buyers. He came into the stationers daily to transmit a document or two and to pick up any communication that was addressed to him.

One day he plopped a lumpy burlap sack on the counter. Powdery dust filtered through the threads of the bag. "Try these," he said. "They are Yukon Gold potatoes. A new variety. A gourmet potato that is a cross between a North American white potato and a South American yellow-fleshed variety."

The Yukon Gold was the beginning of an equitable barter.

"I'll send and receive faxes for PG Potato Marketing."

"I'll bring you sacks of potatoes."

The staff at Chandler Stationers ate well during the summers Paul Grub dickered in spuds – baked potatoes, mashed potatoes, scalloped potatoes, potato salad; red potatoes, white potatoes, russet potatoes and of course the epicurean Yukon Gold.

* * *

Alma Eddleson heard about this amazing fax machine. She needed to send some documents to an attorney in Chicago. He told her to fax them. Alma came in bearing a large manila envelope, sealed, stamped, and addressed to Harry Harbottle, PLC, Chicago. She handed the envelope to Jeff and asked him to fax it to Harry.

"I need to have the documents," Jeff told Alma.

"They're none of your business," said Alma.

"We can't fax an envelope like this," said Jeff. "You'll have to take the papers out of the envelope in order for us to fax them."

"Humpf," snorted Alma. She was not ready for her

personal matters to be sent unshielded through cyber space. "I'll send it myself."

She took her sealed and stamped envelope and dropped it in the post box on the corner.

Chapter 15

CHRISTMAS GREETINGS

"Thirtenly, Mithuth Buthtard, you can pick up your Chwithmath Cardth tomowwow." Viktor finalized Annabelle Bustard's order. I groaned. Before long Annabelle's baby would be talking more clearly than Viktor.

Annabelle Bustard had spent the better part of an hour deciding which Christmas cards she was going to send this year. This was a special Christmas because Annabelle and Jim had a new little baby. They wanted to inform friends and relatives of the addition to their family via their Christmas cards. They had to get the cards out early because the majority of their greetings would go to England.

Jim Bustard had come from Liverpool to study physics at U.C. Davis. There he met Annabelle. They were married right after Jim picked up his diploma. Jim worked for a while at Lockheed, but decided that his real love was teaching. He now was teaching math and physics at the local junior college.

Bustard. Annabelle was proud of the name she had married into. Zdobylak, her maiden name, was a mouthful. Besides putting her at the end of any class list alphabetically, it was unpronounceable as well as difficult to spell. That awkward Polish name had clung to her family since Borys Zdobylak had immigrated to America in 1917.

Bustard was of Anglo-Saxon origin. It originally was a name for a person who had facial features similar to a buzzard. As a matter of fact, Jim was rather buzzard-like in demeanor. Tall, gaunt, and sharp-featured, Jim had a prominent beak nose that protruded from under the bridge of his horn-rimmed spectacles.

Annabelle and James Bustard. Annabelle enjoyed inscribing their names on envelopes. And now there was one-month-old James Junior, Jamie they called him.

Annabelle had decided on a Christmas card with a Victorian motif. Boughs of holly and ivy framed a cheerful doorway on the front of the card. Heavily embossed with glitter and gilt, the message read:

Merry Christmas to your home

Through the glassine windows on the door you could see a classic English family sitting in front of a cheerful hearth. Mother, father, and baby swathed in bunting. When opened, the card read:

From ours

and Viktor was going to personalize the cards for Mrs. Bustard.

With an apparatus called a Kingsley Hot Foil Stamping Machine we imprinted messages on greeting cards, invitations, and stationery. We also personalized Bibles, albums, and leather products such as briefcases and folios. During the Christmas season Viktor sat at the stamping machine almost every day personalizing orders left with him.

Viktor might have had an annoying lisp that affected his verbal communication, but he was quite an ace with our Kingsley Machine. He had done imprinting for the stationery store for years and years. He had a sense of how hot the machine should get for the various foils that were used as well as how much pressure to exert on the lever, and how long to hold the lever down to get precise images. Viktor also had the ability to read various fonts upside down and backwards which was necessary for setting the type. His results were clean, clear, and handsome. We were content to leave this task to Viktor.

Viktor set up the machine during a lull in business during the afternoon. It took a while for the machine to reach the temperature needed for embossing gold foil. Four orders this day awaited him. Packard Farms needed one hundred cards embossed. Other orders were more modest. Every order required a special set-up, a different font, a different color of foil, and of course a different message. Custom embossing was a labor intensive task and one that required concentration. Last on Viktor's agenda was Mrs. Bustard's order. By the time we locked the doors for the evening Viktor had stamped her final card.

Annabelle was anxious to address the cards she would be sending abroad, so she was at the counter early the next day.

"Here you are, Mithuth Buthtard. Your cardth are ready for you." Viktor pulled a package from our special order shelf.

Annabelle eagerly opened the top box to examine the workmanship.

Merry Christmas to your home
From ours

The card read just as Mrs. Bustard expected.
Then she paled. The gold embossed personalization continued:

Annabelle, Jim
and Jamie,
Our new little Bastard

Chapter 16

LEGALEZE

"I'll file the legal forms," I munificently offered. A parcel had just arrived from A-Z Legal Forms, Inc., the publisher of do-it-yourself legal forms and kits. By late afternoon, endless trips around the store assisting customers, unpacking merchandise, and stocking shelves had taken its toll. In spite of my sensible crepe-soled shoes, my legs were weary and my feet hurt. Replenishing the legal form cabinets would at least be a sit-down job.

A bank of two-drawer filing cabinets in a front corner of the store was stocked with over three hundred standard legal forms that could be executed by the customer – forms relating to business, debt, real estate, employment, liability. In addition, complete kits for the gnarlier ordeals of life were available – wills, trusts, divorces, annulments, guardianships, bankruptcies.

No longer did a person have to contact an attorney in order to conduct a simple legal transaction. Chandler Stationers was on the ground floor of selling self-service legal documents to the public. I had procured a Notary Public Commission and was able to provide the service of notarizing important documents of life – affidavits, quit claim deeds, promissory notes, powers of attorney.

Sometimes we found ourselves privy to the personal and financial lives of our customers. We usually did not know the beginning of the story nor the end. Our small role was a vignette somewhere in the middle.

* * *

The Sew & Sew set up business in a small storefront on the square. Sales and service on a line of imported sewing machines was the proprietor's primary trade, however they were also set up to give sewing lessons on these specialty machines. The owners were a young couple from England, Beatrice and Winston, who brought a bit of class to the neighborhood with their refined British accents.

"Easy terms, *Hire Purchase*" a sign in the Sew & Sew window proclaimed. We had to be educated that "Hire Purchase" was their way of saying "Installment Plan."

The Sew & Sew carried a small selection of unique fabrics – heavy Irish linens, soft merino wools, cotton piques of rich and varied hues – a cut above what came off the bolts at the J. C. Penney's dry goods counter. The shop was attractively, if sparsely, stocked. It had a display of sewing notions, *bits and bobs* they called them – needles and pins, hooks and snaps, thimbles and thread – as well as scissors imported from Germany.

Beatrice could make her demo machine sing, and beautifully pleated and tucked garments rolled out from under the needle. These marvelous machines could appliqué, monogram, ruffle, or embroider by clamping on one of a myriad of attachments designed for the special task. Like a car, these sensitive sewing machines needed regular tune-ups. Winston was the service man, the man who oiled and lubricated, cleaned and adjusted tension, in other words kept the machines humming.

Winston would also service other brands of sewing machines, but that was obviously a stop-gap measure to bring in a modicum of income to the new business.

"I'll give it a *jiggery-pokery*," he said when I asked if he would service my reliable Singer.

Beatrice and Winston stepped tenuously into the business life of the square. They nodded politely when they passed on the street. "*Cheerio*," they said. They attended one or two merchants' breakfast meetings, but since their store did not open until mid-morning the early-hour breakfast was not convenient to their business life. *"Too blimey early,"* Winston said.

If I stopped in their store mid-afternoon Beatrice invited, *"Have a cuppa with me, luv?"* On a two-burner hot plate she heated a kettle of water to the boiling point, and then poured it into a china tea pot. Tea was served in translucent Wedgewood cups.

Beatrice sat at her sewing machine day after day stitching smocked baby dresses and suits with flat felled seams. When the garments were finished they hung in the store as samples of what could be created with this marvelous machine.

Beatrice and Winston had sunk their savings into a little part of the American Dream, the dream of having a business of their own – a business that used their talents, a business that promoted quality merchandise, a business that produced beautiful things. They threw their lot into a small store on the Chandler town square.

Winston came into the store late one Saturday afternoon. *"'Tis nowt but a bugger,"* he complained. "This was our last day. We are closing the Sew & Sew. I need to buy a *Bankruptcy Kit*."

* * *

Hilda Graham was not pleased when her daughter Stacy eloped with Jack What's-his-name. "She's only known him for a month," Hilda moaned three days after the deed was done.

I recalled Stacy from when she was in high school, a slightly overweight lass relegated to braces to correct a slight overbite. Lank brown hair framed a face plagued with occasional eruptions of teen-age acne. Sometimes Stacy stopped by the store on her way home from school to purchase refill paper for her notebook or index cards for an upcoming term paper. She seemed to be a conscientious student, but one on the fringe of the social world of her peers.

Hilda wanted Stacy to enroll in the community

college when she finished high school. Stacy, instead, shed her braces as well as a few pounds, had her hair styled at Cassandra's Beauty Plus, and got a job on the assembly line of a local electronics firm. In truth this was a pretty good job for a high school graduate. Stacy was probably twenty years old by now and was enjoying a bit of social life that she had missed in high school.

Jack What's-his-name drifted into town with a case full of brushes, cleaning products, personal care items, and nutritional supplies. When he set out to mark his territory, the Graham's doorbell was the first one in town that he had pushed. Stacy, who answered the door, was intrigued by his miraculous diet pills. She ordered some to insure that those hard-lost pounds from high school stayed off. Jack, then, plied Stacy with a sack full of samples of shampoo, toothpaste, hand creams, dish detergent, and furniture polish. A romance was sparked.

"Love at first sight," the rapturous couple proclaimed.

Jack, who was handsome in a dark unctuous way, delivered a convincing prattle of his prospects as a representative for a nationwide home products company. He would recruit other salesmen to buy into the company and do the leg-work of selling the goods. They, in turn, would enlist others. As each tier was in place, Jack would rise in the business. Before long, he would simply sit back and rake in the profits.

With opportunities manifest, the young couple saw no need to delay matrimony.

Meanwhile . . . until Jack got on his feet . . .

Stacy emptied her modest savings account to help fund a week of postnuptial bliss in honeymoon heaven, Las Vegas.

A month after the hasty JP affair Hilda was in the store again. "Stacy is going to need this," she said. "That smarmy bastard had a wife in El Centro – a wife he walked out on two years ago – but, nevertheless, a lawfully wedded wife!"

She placed an *Annulment* packet on the counter.

* * *

They were an odd-lot strolling into Chandler Stationers. One was tall, lean, and severe. A pencil-thin mustache outlined his upper lip. He looked as if he had stepped off of a movie set. He was dressed in khaki. A loosely belted safari jacket topped a pair of jodhpurs. These wide-hipped pants were met at the knees by tight-fitting black boots. A risqué black beret perched cockily on his well-groomed head.

His companion was short, fat, and disheveled. A day or two of unshaved stubble swathed his face from ear to ear. Rumpled white pants, a yellow ascot tucked loosely at the throat of a blue blazer, and on his head was a similar brimless beret, this one red.

They requested a *DBA* (Doing Business As) form and needed my notary service. The official title of the form was *Affidavit of Trade Name Use*. Many businesses operated under a trade name or a fictitious business name. It simply meant that the name they did business under was not the legal name of the person (or persons) responsible for the business. As a matter of fact, our own store name was a DBA.

These guys proceeded to fill in the form under my nose.

> *State of Arizona*
> *County of Maricopa*
> *We the undersigned . . .* **Walt Disney** *and*
> **Cecile B. DeMille . . .**
> *are the owners of the business firm*
> *doing business under the trade name of*
> **Call Waiting** *. . .*

Whoa! Something was off-key here. Walt Disney! Cecile B. DeMille! Call Waiting! Walt Disney and Cecile B.

DeMille, motion picture moguls, were long dead.

The men whipped out seemingly authentic California Drivers' licenses with their purported identities confirmed. I cocked an eyebrow.

"What's with the names?" I asked.

"We are favored descendents of our illustrious relatives," Mr. Safari expounded.

Should I or shouldn't I notarize the forms? I shrugged my shoulders, verified that the signatures matched the IDs that they had produced. I, then, meticulously recorded the suspicious driver's license details in my notary log and charged the eccentric duo for the service.

Had I just given a stamp of legitimacy to a call-girl service?

Chapter 17

MELA C. LAVARON

"Isn't that Mrs. LaVaron?" I whispered to Jeff.

"It sure is," Jeff growled.

Mrs. LaVaron looked good for her age. She had to be at least fifty-five years old, but she dressed like an eighteen-year-old – plunging neckline, bare midriff, hip-hugging capris. If a strand of grey had infiltrated her scalp it was skillfully disguised in a flaming chestnut mane that tumbled over her shoulders.

And Mrs. LaVaron had the figure to pull it off. Her well-toned physique was the result of countless hours at the spa, treadmilling, cycling, toning her abs and buns. From a distance she looked like a well-stacked college girl. Only when you came nearer were you aware that excessive hours under the sunlamp created a leather-like tone to her skin. Even Botox treatments and a mask of Mary Kaye concealer did not fully disguise the crow's feet emanating from the corners of her eyes or the dewlaps developing under her jaw line. Secretly, I admired Mrs. LaVaron. She was in good shape for the shape she was in. I hoped that I would look as good when I was fifty-five.

Mrs. LaVaron often appeared on the society page of the *Chandler Arizonan*. She and her husband were frequent attendees at galas held at the San Marcos Hotel. Inevitably she was the lady in the picture wearing a spangly form-fitting dinner dress. She actually looked a lot like Rita Hayworth of cinema fame, and I suspected that in her dreams Mrs.

LaVaron equated herself to the glamorous film star.

Today, she strutted through the door on the arm of a handsome hunk of a man who was probably twenty years her junior. The stranger held Mrs. LaVaron's arm possessively. Tall, sensuous, the man had deep-set dark eyes and bronze skin. His hair was thick and black but well-cut. A razor thin mustache outlined his upper lip. He wore crisp white linen pants. His muscles rippled under the tight blue polo shirt that he wore, and a heavy mat of black chest hair was visible through his open collar.

"Do you suppose he's the boat captain?" I hissed.

"Who knows?" Jeff was not going to contribute to the rumor mill.

As Mrs. LaVaron and her companion approached the front counter she flashed a Pepsodent smile. "Hello, again," she said to me. "I have been away for awhile."

Oh, I knew that.

She paused and fluttered her fringed lashes at the man beside her. "This is my friend, Capitan Vicente."

That answered my question.

* * *

We hadn't seen Mrs. LaVaron for over a year, but the scandal was still fresh.

Robert LaVaron was a prominent attorney in Chandler. His lucrative legal practice focused on family law. Many citizens of Chandler laid bare their personal and financial lives in the office of Robert LaVaron where wills and trusts were documented. The nitty-gritty of divorces, annulments, guardianships, adoptions, and custody issues were hammered out in his inner sanctum.

LaVaron PLC maintained an active charge account at the store. Although most supplies for the office were purchased by his secretary, Robert LaVaron occasionally stepped into the store to get a refill for his Montblanc pen. And Mrs. LaVaron made regular purchases of decorative bric-a-brac for their sprawling ranch-style home in the gated

San Marcos neighborhood. When Mrs. LaVaron charged an item at the store she scrawled "Mela C" across the bottom of the sales slip.

Mela LaVaron, the name actually rolled over your tongue in a melodic cadence. Once when Mrs. LaVaron signed her sales slip "Mela C" I asked, "What does the C stand for?" I was just making idle conversation. I thought the C probably represented her maiden name.

She winked at me conspiratorially. "My given name is Irmela Cosette. Can you imagine giving a little baby such a moniker? Robert has always called me Mela C."

A distinguished gentleman, Robert LaVaron was nearing retirement age. Steel grey hair, bifocal glasses, he was the epitome of a prosperous attorney. Although he tended to be on the portly side, he carried his heft well. He apparently did not work out at the spa with the same rigor as his wife. When you saw the LaVarons as a couple you might assume at first glance that the lady had a sugar daddy. But Robert LaVaron seemed to enjoy escorting the glamorous Mela C.

Once the counselor told me that he would like to spend half the year at his beach home in Guaymas, Mexico. He and Mela C. made several trips a year to the seaport town south of the border where he kept in dock a luxury cabin cruiser called *Mela C. LaVaron* after you-know-who. Sailing through the straits of Baja California was Robert LaVaron's notion of a perfect retirement. The LaVarons seemed to have the best of all worlds: money, a grandiose home in Chandler, a Mexican hacienda, and a vessel to transport them through the twilight of their years.

One morning Jeff and I were finishing breakfast. I had hustled Heather and Beth off to school in a flurry of notebooks, backpacks, and musical instruments. Part of the morning rush was gone. Our pre-schooler, Katie, had toddled off to her room. The house was momentarily quiet. It was time to send Jeff on to work, but we dallied over the morning newspaper and a second cup of coffee. I would be staying home this day to post accounts receivable in the ledger.

"My gosh, Jeff, did you see this!" I pointed to an article buried in the second section of the *Arizona Republic*. Of course he hadn't. Jeff was reading the Letters to the Editor.

"Prominent Chandler Attorney Dies in Guaymas" was the headline. "Robert LaVaron, Chandler attorney, drowned in the straits of Baja California. . ." Robert LaVaron and his wife, Mela C. LaVaron, were spending the Easter holidays at their beach home in Guaymas. On Saturday they had taken their boat into the Gulf of California. Accompanying them on this excursion was a friend, Capitan Norberto Vicente, who owned a small tour company in Guaymas. Capitan Vicente scheduled tourist excursions and fishing trips aboard his own vessels moored at the same dock where the LaVaron's harbored their cabin cruiser. The story went on to say that unexplained circumstances surrounded the lawyer's death. "Robert LaVaron, an accomplished sailor. . . The weather was mild. . . The waters calm. . ."

"Tsk, tsk, tsk," I muttered. "What a terrible accident."

"At least he was doing something he loved to do," Jeff replied.

Of course, nobody knew what went on aboard the *Mela C. LaVaron*. But various people around town had their own ideas.

Following Robert LaVaron's funeral, Mrs. Daniels came into the store. The Daniels lived next door to the LaVarons. Dick Daniels owned the General Motors agency in town. It was through him that the LaVarons got the sleek Cadillac Eldorado convertible that Mela drove.

"Dear Robert," Mrs. Daniels sighed. "He gave that woman anything her heart desired. Why, just last month they were looking at the new Cadillac models. Mela had her sights set on the Seville. Robert was ready to place an order."

Another customer said, "Mela is a looker, all right. Robert should have kept her on a tighter rein."

And another, "You have to wonder. Robert knew how

to handle a boat."

Andy Aikers, the Benefit Life Insurance representative in town, said, "Having a wife like that, something was bound to happen. You can believe that we are investigating the situation."

The Mela C. LaVaron

But Felicia Ruiz had the last word. Felicia had worked for the LaVarons for ten years. She was originally from Guaymas which suggested that the LaVarons might have first known her south of the border. How legitimate her work documents were I couldn't say. In a region teeming with undocumented workers one didn't ask.

Every day, Monday through Friday, Felicia walked from her home on the east side of town to her job where she washed windows, scoured bathrooms, vacuumed carpets, polished silver, and dusted crystal chandeliers. She even worked up to doing a bit of cooking and serving, especially if the LaVarons were having a to-do. And when the LaVarons were out of town Felicia stayed in a back bedroom to watch the house and feed Rusty, the LaVaron's Irish Setter.

Several days after the funeral Felicia was in the store to buy a Spanish birthday card to send to an aunt in her home country. She was unusually subdued as she paid for her purchase. I wondered if she would be able to keep her job considering the unfortunate circumstances.

"*¡Dios mío!*" she exclaimed after we commented on the death of her employer. "I knew that the señor made a mistake when he named that boat. *Iay!* A bad mistake! That boat was a curse!"

"Why was the boat a curse?" I was puzzled.

"*¡Una profecía!* It was a prophecy! The boat that he christened Mela C. LaVaron was a prophecy! In Spanish the name reads *me la clavaron!*" Felicia walked out of the store shaking her head.

I hastened to pick up a Spanish dictionary from our book shelf.

Me la clavaron?

Clavar: to nail, to screw, to swindle.

Mela C. LaVaron

Me la clavaron! "I was screwed!"

Chapter 18

THE OSTRICH FESTIVAL

Chandler hosted a series of festivals intended to draw the community together for fun and profit. Merchants on the square were lured into the revelries and encouraged to set up tables outside their stores and hawk their wares.

Each festival was heralded by a community parade around the square. Boy Scout Troop 76 carried the colors, and men standing along the route doffed their truckers' caps and Stetsons to honor the flag. The mayor waved benignly from the back seat of a Cadillac convertible provided by Dick Daniels' Dealership. The high school band, in turn, maintained quasi formation as it honked and hooted around the corners. Pom pom girls flounced and rattled crepe paper bouquets to the beat of the school fight song. The Homecoming Queen and King, donned in formal regalia and cardboard crowns, beamed from another convertible donated by Daniels. Future Farmers of America straddled bales of hay on a wagon pulled by a John Deere tractor. Little girls from JoElla's Dance studio pranced about in sequined leotards. Other community organizations followed: Mary Maguire's Brownie Troop, two goats led by employees of Dillon's Goat farm, the Rough Riders motorcycle jockeys, and a series of horses followed by pooper scooper clowns.

The first community celebration that we participated in after we moved onto the square was Maxwell Street Days. The Chandler gala was patterned after an old Chicago tradition that drew people to Maxwell Street, purported to have biggest open-air market in the nation. On Maxwell Street in Chicago, clothes, produce, appliances, tools – virtually anything anyone might want – was available at greatly discounted prices. Maxwell Street Days in Chandler was a watered-down version of its namesake event. We hoped to unload our marketing disasters of the previous year.

Saba's hauled out dungarees, shirts, and kerchiefs that had been rejected by the shopping populace.

The drug store brought out combs, brushes, and barrettes from an outmoded coiffure display.

The hardware store featured orphan mixing bowls and spatulas.

Chandler Stationers jumped into the mood of festivities by bringing to the street bins of mismatched party plates and napkins, boxes of shelf-worn stationery and faded photo albums. Needless to say, the shopping public was not lured by our merchandising ploy. Generally Maxwell Street Days was an exercise in weeding out stock and donating unsellable product to the Salvation Army Thrift Store.

Other festivals aimed at revitalizing the spirit of Chandler followed. Chandler Days was an attempt at recreating Chandler history. Period costumes and vintage vehicles were added to the parade.

Then came Doo Dah Days, with a parade roster lined with absurd antics by Stilt Walkers, a Briefcase Brigade, a Lawn Chair Drill Team, and local pretty boys dressed in drag.

But nothing rivaled the next marketing brainstorm of the city fathers. The Ostrich Festival.

In the early years of the 20th Century, ostrich feathers became fashion accessories. When horse and carriage was the mode of transportation, ladies of style strutted their stuff under capacious bonnets of fluffy ostrich feathers. During the height of ostrich plume fashion, several Chandler entrepreneurs determined that the desert Southwest was as good a place as South Africa to raise ostriches. Chandler became home to several ostrich farms that provided feathers to a world-wide market.

The Ostrich Festival would be a tribute to those days in Chandler history and would hopefully bring visitors to the town. In addition to standard parade entries a herd of ostriches would march down the street. At the park, in addition to hotdogs, and cotton candy, ostrich burgers and ostrich barbecue would be served. In addition to stuffed pandas and plastic pin wheels, ostrich feather fans and boas would be sold. Ostrich leather gloves, ostrich leather boots, ostrich leather purses, ostrich eggs. Everything was coming up ostrich.

* * *

Monte McCrea was a cowboy of some note around Chandler. He had the basic skills of many rodeo cowboys – bull riding, calf roping, chute dogging. However he took top honors in western rodeos in bareback bronc riding. If anyone could bring a bucking bronco to his knees it was Monte McCrea.

Monte was a little rangy guy. He probably didn't weigh more than 135 pounds soaking wet. When he wasn't following the western rodeo circuit he was riding fence for the Grummel Brothers. A fellow with Monte's dexterity as well as his know-how of horses and cattle was in high demand on cattle ranches in the area.

Preparations for the Ostrich Festival were in full swing across the street in the park when Monte swaggered into the store. He doffed his felt Stetson as he greeted the ladies at the counter.

"Ladies," he nodded as he passed the cash register.

He seemed to have come from the barber shop next door. He smelled of Ivory soap and Old Spice. A startling demarcation appeared across the back of his neck. Roughened sun-burned skin above his collar and a ring of pale white chicken-skin where his newly shorn hair had been

Monte was dressed for an afternoon on the town. He wore a classic pearl-buttoned western shirt and a turquoise nugget bolo tie.

He walked with a somewhat pinched and crab-like stride. High-heeled pointy-toed boots might have helped him stay in the saddle, but Monte couldn't walk a straight line if he had to. He had the classic bow legs and skinny butt of a guy who spent his life on a horse. A pair of well-worn Levis was held up by a tooled leather belt sporting a trophy buckle the size of a dinner plate. A signature tobacco tin formed a circle in his right rear pocket.

"Hello, Monte." Jeff looked up from a display of staplers he was in the process of arranging on the shelves. "What can we do for you?"

"There's sure a lot goin' on about this-here ostrich festival." Monte replied.

"Yeah. More falderal than good sense," Jeff said. "After they block the streets we can count on no business for the next two days. Festival goers will be here for the parade and the frolic. Regular customers won't fight the crowds to get in."

"I guess there's a down side to everything," Monte acknowledged.

"But, hey! I have a display of ostrich eggs on the counter," Jeff continued. "Blown ostrich eggs, of course. I got them from a guy who raises ostriches in New Mexico." Jeff pointed to a laundry basket with six soccer ball sized orbs nesting in it. "Ten dollars each, they are."

"They would make a helluv 'n omelet," Monte responded. Then he pulled a folded paper from his shirt pocket. "Look at this."

An orange handbill featured a cartoon ostrich. It read: "Ostrich races Saturday afternoon. Ride an ostrich to the finish line. Prizes. Sign up at festival headquarters. Tent #17."

"I'm gonna give this a whirl," Monte said. It can't be any harder than ridin' a bronc."

"And the ostrich will have a saddle," Jeff joshed.

* * *

Ostrich is God's little joke on the animal kingdom. When He divvied up the creatures of the world into birds and beasts, Ostrich did not know which line to step into. Because of Ostrich's indecision God made a caricature of grand size that straddled both genera. His creation had long legs propelling him in the gait of a camel and a long bare neck linking him with sauropods of the dinosaur age. Adorning this parody of animation was a ruffle of lacy feathers pretty enough for a lady's Sunday bonnet. A giant among birds, Ostrich is also the most foolish of birds; his eye is bigger than his brain; he can neither fly nor sing. God placed Ostrich in the desert expanse of South Africa to live. Since the time of creation Ostrich has migrated around the world, but he flourishes in hot, dry places. Chandler, Arizona is perfect Ostrich habitat.

* * *

Nothing could have kept us away from the ostrich races on Saturday afternoon. The races themselves were held on a dusty lot a few blocks from the other festival activities. We sat hunched on the portable grandstand with a hundred or so other curious spectators squinting into the sun and wiping sweat from our brows. Even in March the hot sun beat down on the Arizona desert.

Most of the ostrich jockeys were employees of the ostrich farms although that fact was not publicized. We, of course, were there to cheer for our local untried hero.

Monte met his assigned mount, Lady Rosebud, before the race commenced. Rosie, as she was called, batted her seductive long lashes and ruffled her bustle. Then a little white sock was popped over her head as four similarly blind-folded ostriches were led to adjoining chutes. The blindfolds kept them relatively calm. Ostriches are prone to panic, but seem to subscribe to the notion that what they can't see isn't happening. Their long necks arched and waved over the bars. A signal was given. The riders mounted their charges from the chute fences. Lacy feather wings were pulled back and draped over the riders' thighs. A second signal was given.

84

Blindfolds were pulled and the gates opened simultaneously.

Monte, astride Rosebud, bolted beyond the fence. He had abandoned his felt cowboy hat for a cyclist helmet strapped tightly under his chin. The aim of the game was to get the bird out the gate and around the track to the finish line. Staying on the bird was an integral part of the sport. With no halter or directional device to signal to the bird which way to go, this was a monumental feat. Five feather dusters bumped and jostled and wove around one another in an orchestrated ballet. Oops, one jockey, loosing his grip, slid down the back of his bird, landed on the dusty track, and rolled to the side just in time to avoid being impaled by his mount's hoary talon.

Rosebud had a half-mind of her own and part way through the dance she did an about face and headed back toward the chutes. Then, just as abruptly, Rosebud began doing solo pirouettes in the arena. Round and round she whirled, her feathers fluffed majestically. Monte, white-knuckled, gripped the base of Rosebud's wings. Other contestants, not to be left out of this choreography, turned despite their riders' protests, and began running circles around the demented dervish. Their knobby necks twisted and undulated like snakes. "Ring around Rosie." The old children's nursery rhyme came to mind.

Another jockey lost his seat. And another. Race officials scurried about the arena corralling ostriches gone amok. The race was still on for Monte and his remaining opponent. But neither bird seemed inclined to head toward the finish line. Rosie, tired of her dizzying spin resumed her lope back to the chutes.

Monte managed to stay on his mount but ended up back at the starting point. The other bird turned maniacally and raced toward the spectators deposing his rider in the process. Then he turned and lamely wandered over the finish line. I didn't know if an ostrich crossing the finish line without his rider was a legitimate win. The whole event lasted less than three rollicking minutes.

A week later we saw Monte again. The trappings of the Ostrich Festival were gone. The only reminder of the event was the six ostrich eggs that we had hoped to sell. They remained nestled in a laundry basket near the front counter. Just what would a person do with an ostrich egg anyway?

"Well, Cowboy," Jeff greeted him. "Are you changing your rodeo specialty?"

"Nah," Monte replied. "I'll leave those homicidal giant chickens with their keepers."

Chapter 19

SERVICE WITH A SMILE

"We will stand behind anything we sell," Dad boasted. Thus we were pretty lenient in our Exchanges and Returns policy.

When Mae Lewellen discovered that the paper plates and napkins she bought for her P.E.O. social clashed with her upholstery, she exchanged them for a pattern that had more mauves and lavenders. When Betty Benson received two wedding albums at her shower, she exchanged one album for a pearl-handled knife and cake server to use at her wedding reception. When Henry Langaard did not like the way his list finder operated, we gave him his money back. We knew our merchandise, and we were not hung up on requiring proof-of-purchase or receipts.

However, once I balked at giving a refund on a Bible.

A stranger met me half-way down the aisle. The gentleman was pleasant-looking. He wore neatly creased grey slacks, a starched white shirt with a conservative tie knotted at his throat. His grey hair was neatly trimmed and his shoes shined. He might have just stepped out of Sunday Services at the Episcopal Church, except it was Thursday.

"Are you Susan?" he asked.

"Yes."

"The lady at the cash register told me to talk to you."

"Oh."

"My wife purchased this Bible for me. A gift for our 40th Anniversary."

In his hand was one of our Bibles, a Cambridge Bible, a beautiful leather-bound edition, thumb-indexed, its pages edged in gold.

"It so happens that I have a very similar leather Bible. I would like to return this one for a refund." He smiled benignly.

We originally had had two copies of this particular Bible. Mrs. Applegate purchased one at Christmas time, a special gift for her son who would enter Princeton Seminary in the fall. The other Bible should still be on the shelf.

"When was your wife in the store?" I asked the gentleman. I took the book from his outstretched hand. The price sticker was still on the bottom of the box. Fifty-five dollars was a whopping amount to pay for a Bible in those days. Would his wife leave a price tag on a gift?

"I believe she was here last week," he replied.

I made an uncharacteristic decision. "Do you have a receipt?" I asked.

"It's in the car." The man did an about-face and left the store.

As I suspected, he did not return.

I returned the Bible to the shelf where a tell-tale rim of dust indicated the spot where the Bible had lain before our sanctimonious customer pilfered it and tried to get a refund.

* * *

Gus Gorby was a good ole boy. He dealt in real estate, mostly farm and land exchanges. Gus always appeared this side of seedy. Maybe farm appraisers did not have to be sartorially astute. His dark hair, peppered with grey, brushed the collar of a wrinkled white shirt. His black shoes were scuffed, his socks mismatched. Pleated tan pants hitched above his waist with a cracked leather belt gave Gus a Humpty Dumpty look.

"I'm afraid that the lead in this pencil does not extend smoothly," Gus said. He laid a Parker pencil on the counter. Viktor had spent an hour with the man last week showing him all the mechanical pencils in the store. "I'd like to have my money back"

"Thertainly Guth. Thervith with a thmile ith our motto. Thatithfakthion guawanteed.

Gus took Viktor's proclamation to heart.

"I've discovered that I do not care for this self-anchoring pencil sharpener." Gus smiled apologetically. We refunded $15.99 plus tax on the pencil sharpener.

"My wife found another expense book in the desk drawer." Back came a Budget and Income Tax Record book.

"The digits on this calculator are hard to read." We returned his money on a handheld calculator.

Every time Gus Gorby walked in the door he was bringing back something he had purchased. He was always polite, apologetic, and self-effacing.

"I do not need this box of file folders."

"These scissors . . ."

"This desk pad . . ."

"This roll of Scotch Tape . . ."

"Thkoth tape! Who ever returned a forty-nine thent woll of thkoth tape?"

Gus Gorby did. It became a joke with us to see when old Gus would return his most recent purchase.

Well, Gus Gorby needed a paper shredder. The personal shredders that we had in stock were not to his liking.

"I need a commercial paper shredder," Gus said.

He poured over our catalog and settled on a heavy-duty model, a cross-cut shredder with start/stop paper feed, one that would take twenty sheets of paper in one bite, one that would gobble staples, one with a reverse function. It required a special order.

The shredder arrived in our mid-week product delivery van.

Gus picked up the paper shredder on a Friday afternoon.

Monday morning he walked in the door. Sure enough. He was bearing the carton containing the paper shredder.

"Unfortunately this is not adequate for my needs," Gus apologized.

I opened the box to check out the returning merchandise. The teeth of the shredder were lined with paper dust. A few glittery staple bits were stuck in its tracks.

I casually commented to Gus. "Did you finish your project?"

"Oh, yes. Got it done," he replied. "It took me all weekend, but I got it done."

I sighed and reached for a sales book to record another return.

Chapter 20

A FAMILY AFFAIR

The last week of the year could only be described as frantic. First we had to de-Christmas the store. For a few days we sold Christmas gift wrap, boxed cards, and holiday baubles for half-price. The matrons of the community rushed in to get a jump on seasonal decorations for the following year. Surrounded by the fallout of the Yule we unstrung garlands of plastic holly, counted what was left of the ceramic Santas and tinsel angels, and packed Hallmark Christmas cards for teacher, grandmother, sweetheart, and neighbor in storage boxes for another year.

New products began arriving. Businesses, gearing up for tax season, purchased binders and filing systems, ledgers and account books, appointment books and calendars. This was also heavy tourist season. Vacationers staying at the San Marcos Hotel drifted in to purchase regional post cards, souvenirs, and western books.

Amid this bedlam we were supposed to conduct inventory. The IRS required retail establishments operating on a fiscal year beginning January 1st to report stock on hand as of the 31st of December.

All hands were on deck to count the contents of the store – clerks, stock boys, plus a smattering of high school kids hired on a temporary basis. Jeff armed the troops with clip boards, yellow columnar pads, and #2 Ticonderoga pencils. Each inventory taker was assigned a section of shelving. The task was to record every item on those shelves, clamps, clips, collators, compasses, curves.

Bar codes and laser scanners would be innovations of the future to keep track of inventory. We were locked into an archaic unary numeral system, tally, tally, tally, tally, hash mark; tally, tally, tally, tally, hash mark. Thus we worked our way through address books, adhesives, badges, binders, blotters, business forms . . . calendars, calculators, carbon paper, card files, composition books . . . envelopes, erasers, fasteners, folders. . . paper, pencils, pens, portfolios . . . scissors, scrapbooks, sorters, stencils . . . In spite of what the IRS expected, this was not a one-day, 31st of December job. The tedious task went on and on through January as we attended to customers and geared up for Valentine's Day which was another red letter season on the business calendar.

From the time our children were old enough to count to ten they were expected to help with inventory. Eleven-year-old Heather was quite capable of lining up an array of staplers by model number and recording needed information in designated columns on her legal pad. Eight-year-old Beth tallied boxes of file folders and reams of mimeograph paper. Even five-year-old Katie was set to counting the gum erasers. She dumped a basket of erasers on the floor then stacked the rubber blocks into towers of ten. Someone else could come along and compute the score.

At the end of it all, a boatload of legal pads swamped my desk daring me to make sense of the columns of gibberish. I defied the IRS to challenge our system.

* * *

The children were also called to the front when festivals occurred. Maxwell Street Days, Chandler Days, The Doo Dah Festival, The Ostrich Festival – whatever the occasion – Heather, Beth, and Katie stood at a table outside the store and hawked distressed merchandise that we could not sell at full retail. Unlike many children who do not know what their parents do when they drive off to work, our children understood from an early age what Mom and Dad did for a living. And they had the privilege as well as the responsibility of participating in the operation of the store.

Of the three girls, Beth took to the business of merchandising at an early age. Often she spent Saturdays at the store with her father. She usually extorted a deal from him. She would dust and stack the agate files in exchange for a pen from the new display of felt markers. The price was right. The card files were in order. During her childhood tenure, Beth amassed a big collection of writing instruments. Little merchant that she was, Beth took her pencils and pens to school and sold them to her school mates for Double Bubble and Tootsie Rolls until her teacher halted the enterprise.

During a scheduled conference with Beth's teacher I was apprised of the following scenario:

One day Teacher called Beth up to her desk.

Teacher: "Beth, You did not put your name on your math test. Put your name on it right now."

Beth: "May I borrow a pencil?"

Teacher (sternly): "Beth, I can't believe you don't have a hundred pencils in your desk.

Beth returned to her desk, rummaged a bit, and returned to Teacher to sign her math test.

Beth: "Seventy-eight. I only have seventy-eight pencils.

Through the years the girls could always depend on part-time employment at either the Chandler store or the Indian School store. They graduated from working for felt markers to actually being on the payroll.

* * *

"Mail's here," Heather called. "J.C. Penney's." She read the return address on the envelope she held.

"Oh," I murmured. "It's a bill from Penney's."

"Does everybody in the country get a bill from J.C. Penney's today?" Heather asked.

A family affair.

"Not everybody," I replied. "However, thousands of bills must go out of Penney's headquarters daily."

The tidy #6 ¾ envelope with my name and address showing through a two-inch window had obviously been run through a postal meter. The missive that I pulled from the envelope was a tidy communiqué of my monthly transactions at Penney's; packages of socks for the girls, a new pair of shoes for Jeff, several lengths of calico for new school dresses were listed in precise Courier font.

Chandler Stationers had an Edwardian method of dispensing statements. Throughout the month I took the hand-scribbled invoices that accumulated at the cash register and laboriously transcribed them onto our posting system. This tri-level system included a statement, a customer card, and a ledger page, with sheets of carbon paper between each level. If I kept my posting up-to-date throughout the month, by the first day of the following month I was ready to assemble statements to send to our customers.

I often employed the girls to help me with the project. The middle of the living room floor became statement headquarters where we could spread out the accoutrement of accounts receivable – posting tray, stacks of invoices, boxes of envelopes, staplers, and stamps. One by one I removed a statement and card from the posting tray, gave it the once-over to see that it was in order, matched applicable invoices to that statement, and stapled the various sheets together. Beth and Katie folded the stapled assemblies and slid statements into envelopes, carefully checking to be sure the complete address could be read through the glassine window. Heather moistened the envelope flaps, and then affixed an eight-cent stamp to each missive. As our work progressed, envelopes spread over the floor like cards in a game of fifty-two pick-up.

"You say Penney's mails thousands of statements a day?" Heather reminded me of our discussion when she brought our mail in.

She mopped her brow. Although I had provided a moist sponge to secure the envelopes and to adhere the stamps, Heather's little tongue was also at work on the project. Sticky mucilage from the envelopes and stamps coated her tongue and lined her teeth.

She wrinkled her nose and flipped her tongue over parched lips. "Man, I'm glad that I'm not J. C. Penney's kid," she said.

Chapter 21

BEETLE MANIA

The door chime announced her arrival.

"Good morning, Mrs. Strathmore." I greeted her.

Ever since Daniel Strathmore turned the reins of the family farm over to his sons, he had been serving in the Arizona State Senate. While he was busy in budget and finance committees at the state level, his wife was busy in social and charitable committees in the community.

A stern angular woman, today she wore a grey pants suit and a blue silk blouse. Whenever I saw Mrs. Strathmore she looked as if she had just stepped out of Hannah's House of Hair, her short hair sculpted into a grey helmet. As usual she was groomed to perfection, a dusting of face powder over her rouged cheeks, a touch of natural pink on her lips, and a wisp of mascara around her hazel eyes.

Mrs. Strathmore was a gracious but a busy woman. She whipped open her leather Day Runner and enumerated a list of items she needed to purchase.

Today she was on a mission for the Community Club, purchasing paper plates and napkins for an upcoming scholarship tea recognizing outstanding high school girls. Mrs. Strathmore had hosted the annual Community Club tea in her home for the past several years. The theme of her tea reflected the Chandler High School colors, royal blue and white. She knew down to the last plastic fork what she would need for the event.

"We should have twelve girls and their mothers,"

Mrs. Strathmore told me. "Perhaps a few grandmothers will come too. And then there are the members of the Community Club. I will need service for at least fifty guests."

"Plates, napkins, cups?" I confirmed with her.

"No cups," she replied. "I have plenty of glass cups that go with my punch bowl. I will need paper plates and napkins and plastic forks too."

However, before we reached the party goods aisle, a candy basket featured in our china cabinet caught her eye. It was a hand-blown limited-edition piece of art glass from a well-known company. A rich cobalt blue, the elegant basket rested upon a shallow pedestal. Hand-painted flowers and butterflies dotted the fluted rim of the basket, and a ribbon of glass arced over the piece to form a handle.

"How lovely," she exclaimed. "Cerulean. Wouldn't this make a nice accessory to my newly upholstered side chairs? And it is the right color to use as a bon-bon dish for the scholarship tea." In an impulsive and uncharacteristic move, Mrs. Strathmore decided to purchase something that was not on her list.

I took the basket to the check-out counter while Mrs. Strathmore selected paper goods for her soiree. She choose a blue and white floral pattern of napkins and paper plates and left me to assemble the necessary packages while she went about the store collecting a few other items on her list.

We met back at the counter, I with the napkins, plates, and plastic forks, as well as a box to contain the glass basket, she with name tags, felt markers, and a box of blue votives. After tallying her purchase, I pulled a shopping bag from under the counter and opened it to contain the items.

Horror of horrors! Two beetles scurried from the bag over the paper plates and began a mating ritual in the object d'art.

* * *

The invasion of the beetles was underway. Since beetles are the dominant form of life on earth – one in every five living species is a beetle – this was an alarming scenario.

97

Some phenomenon of nature had called the worldly population of bark beetles to the Chandler town square. They were little domed critters, some black and some brown, about the size of a small fingernail. They scurried about on six hoary legs and twitched two spindly antennae. Upon close examination you would see a head flexibly attached to its thorax and two bulbous multifaceted eyes.

The creatures seemed to be migrating from the park and moving in a westerly direction. They were squashed on the street and underfoot on the sidewalk. They crawled up the walls, through cracks in the window sills, and under the doors. They infiltrated every nook and cranny of the store.

Drawers under the counter where we kept sales slips, pencils, and tape harbored untold skittering creatures. Locked display cases might have kept pilfering fingers off the Cross pens and Casio calculators, but they did nothing to deter the pugnacious bugs. Whether we were selling boxes of stationery, packages of alphabetical tabs, columnar pads, coin boxes, clasp envelopes, or index cards we were likely to disturb a beetle silently grinding his fierce little mandibles.

Beetles snuggled into greeting card racks, tubs of erasers, boxes of envelopes, portfolios, and desk trays. They curled up among business forms, and baskets of gift bows. A wave of them permeated the china cabinet and dropped into crystal bowls. They were under the skirts of little Dresden figurines and in boxes of silver wedding cake servers.

* * *

Here I stood at the cash register helping the esteemed senator's wife.

"Yike!" I stomped my foot. A little creature scurried over my toes and up my leg.

Ultimately the beetles migrated to the edges of the shelves, rolled up and died. A week of the pesky little critters and they were gone. At least the live ones were gone, but a major shelf cleaning was in store. For months and even years we found beetle carcasses amid our inventory.

But at the moment two of the little beasties were having a tumble in Her Honor's candy dish.

Mrs. Strathmore cocked an arched brow. She was, after all, the wife of a farmer. "Do the bugs come with the basket?" she asked.

Chapter 22

T FOR TWO

Little League season was underway. After Saturday games conducted on the junior high playing field we'd often see a group of 5th grade boys swaggering down the street sporting uniforms emblazoned with Dunn Right Plumbing. Doug Dunn was the owner of the enterprise that sponsored this group of midget athletes. He was also one of the coaches for the team. Doug was a popular coach. After every game, win or lose, he treated the boys to ice cream cones at the Frosty Freeze.

Thus, I watched Doug and the boys from the front window where I was arranging a new display of china teacups and teapots, items I was featuring for upcoming Mothers' Day. The boys pushed and jostled one another as they licked their cones and replayed every inning of the just-past game. I only hoped that one of the cones didn't plop in the middle of the sidewalk requiring me to retrieve bucket and mop and hasten to clean the sticky mess.

Dewey Dunn was Doug's ten-year-old, one of the key players on the team. He played left field and scurried after balls like a determined retriever. Singularly responsible for getting field balls to second and third base, Dewey set up spectacular outs on the Little League field. Dewey was always front and center of the Dunn Right Plumbing entourage as it blustered down the street. Little Delbert Dunn trailed in their wake. Delbert was six-years-old and he basked in the team's glory when the older boys won a game and agonized in their defeat when they lost a game.

This day, Little Delbert sported his own Dunn Right Plumbing uniform. He was playing on a newly-formed adjunct T-Ball team. Younger boys, five and six years old, played T-Ball before moving up to Little League status. In T-Ball the coach placed the ball on a stand or a tee and allowed the batter to strike at the ball. Hitting off a tee was much easier for younger children than hitting a pitched ball. Once contact was made, the player advanced around the bases while the opposing team tried to make an out. Little Delbert was coming into his own as a ball player.

Doug saw me in the window and waved. His grungy Levis hung precariously around his hips. His faded shirt bore stains from working under Mrs. Pickett's sink that morning. He stopped and watched me as I set the last china teapot on the shelf. As if on impulse, he darted in the door.

"Do you have a T-ball?" he asked.

"T-ball?" I blubbered. "Well, we do have Parker T-Ball Jotter pens."

"Nah, I mean a T-ball."

We were an office supply store and a gift shop. We had T-squares, T-pins, and T-tabs. . . But T-balls?

"Why don't you try the sporting goods store at Ray Road?" I suggested.

"Do you think a sporting goods store is likely to have a T-Ball?"

"More likely than we are."

"Well," Doug said. "I thought you might have one since you were putting new teapots in your window."

"T-ball! Tea ball!" I was enlightened.

A tea ball was a relic of the past. Sometimes called a tea egg or a tea infuser, it was a strainer in which dried tea leaves were placed for steeping in a teapot full of hot water. During the time of Queen Victoria no self respecting British family would be without one. Somehow Doug Dunn, disheveled and reeking of sweat from a hot afternoon on the baseball diamond did not evoke the image of a refined family of the Crown having tea.

"Why, yes . . . I do have a tea ball!"

Indeed, we had several elegant tea balls languishing on a back shelf of the china cabinet along with crystal knife rests and salt cellars, seldom used vestiges of fine dining. This request reminded me that I would have to add the tea balls to my display in the front window.

Do you have a T-ball?

I spread the small assortment of tea balls on the counter for Doug to examine. The porcelain strainers, reminiscent of *Fabergé* eggs, were of two parts that unscrewed to allow insertion of tea leaves. A silver hook and chain attached to the top half of the egg allowed the ball to be removed from the pot of hot water when steeping was complete. Each tea ball came with its own decorated saucer to hold the ball when steeping was complete.

Doug cradled one of the tea balls in his hands. Embellished with violets and filigree, the delicate object was consumed by Doug's great dirty paws.

"I'll take this one," Doug declared. "And wrap it for Mothers' Day."

Chapter 23

THE HOOLIGANS

It took us a while to realize that we were buying a lot more India ink than we were selling. Bottles of permanent drawing ink disappeared from the shelves as soon as it was stocked. It was the same with the finger-balance postal scales. Flat lever devices, these little scales could easily be carried in shirt pockets. In fact some people called them take-along pocket scales. If you didn't do serious postal business, this scale was an economical alternative to the larger Pelouze scales that we sold.

We discovered that these simple office supplies, India ink and finger-balance postal scales, were in high demand by the thugs of Chandler. Even cow-town Chandler had its criminal element.

The ink was used to create tattoos. Rugged images of barbed wire circled biceps and necks. Spider webs laced shoulders and nipples. Menacing daggers, skulls, and snakes curled around arms. An occasional partaker in skin adornment had a teardrop or two tattooed on the side of his face. Although some of the skin art was obviously the work of skilled tattooists, much was the result of back-alley tattooing.

The small postal scales were used to weigh illegal substances that were sold on dark corners and out of sinister vans. An envelope could be clipped to the balance and the little scale would register a weight of up to five ounces, just right for calculating minute drug transactions. We were abetting the criminal element of Chandler!

We talked to the Chief of Police about the issue.

"Tattoos actually help the police keep abreast of gang activity," Chief Brannigan told us. "If a perp is apprehended and charged in some misdemeanor or crime, tattoos usually link him with one of the street gangs."

Ah, so the police were actually up on this element of counter-culture.

Nevertheless, we transferred the ink and postal scales to a drawer under the cash register. Customers needing these products had to request them. A fair number of seedy characters sidled in, circled the pen and ink counter, and finally determined what they were seeking was not on the shelves.

"Do ya got Indja ink?" was a reluctant request. Or "Where's dem finger scales?"

Whereupon we would produce a bottle of waterproof drawing fluid or a little brass weighing device. The products still got into disreputable hands, but at least we got our money out of them.

Psst . . . Do ya got India ink?

When the little scales were finally gone, we did not replace them. Offices in Chandler generally needed postal scales that registered more than five ounces for their business communication anyway. However, we did continue selling the drawing ink from under the counter, for it was a valid art medium.

"Psst . . .Do ya got Indja ink?"

* * *

The walk to the bank was but half-a-block. I made the journey every afternoon about 3:30. Several merchants around the square had a similar routine, wanting to get to the bank before it closed at 4:00. On this day a young man leaning against a pillar of the colonnade appeared to be studying his fingernails. My hackles were instantly raised. I sensed that although his head was down, his eyes were following the parade to the bank. I instinctively pulled the deposit bag closer to my body and veered nearer the buildings.

This young man had the marks of a hooligan right down to a teardrop tattoo under his left eye. He wore baggy black pants loosely secured above his buttocks and a sleeveless white undershirt exposing the tattoo of a fiendish cat across his upper right arm. The hair of this zombie-like feline was spiked in erratic angles as if its tail had been stuck in an electric socket. In ornate Old English script the words El Gato (The Cat) curled over the feline's diabolic head.

Jeff and I referred to this suspicious young man as El Gato. We periodically saw him gliding around the plaza seemingly without purpose. And every so often he materialized in our store selecting times when we were busy and found it difficult to keep him in our radar.

On this day I scurried to the bank without mishap. El Gato was gone when I exited the bank, and I hoped I would not find him in our store.

Weeks passed and another Christmas season was upon us. Suddenly I realized El Gato was in the store. He was perusing holiday cards on a rack near the office.

As I approached, he quickly removed a card from the rack and opened it as if to read the message.

"May I help you?" I pointedly asked.

"I was looking for a Christmas card for my grandmother," he mumbled, and studied the card in his hand assiduously.

My eyes fell on the card he held.

"A Hanukkah card?" I asked in disbelief. A small selection of Hanukkah cards for our Jewish clientele lined the end of the rack. "You plan to give your grandmother a Hanukkah card for Christmas?"

He stuffed the card back in the rack and in true stealth form . . . vanished.

We began to ascribe other nefarious acts to the store as the mark of El Gato.

* * *

Viktor opened the store at 8:00 every morning. Business was light at that early hour, but an occasional rancher or businessman came in before the hubbub of his day began. During this lull Viktor prepared the cash register for the new day and counted money from the previous day's receipts. His desk was at the back of the store, but not actually in the office. This position allowed him to work on orders, yet be available to customers.

The door-bell announced the entrance of a shopper. Viktor tucked the cash bag into the top drawer of the desk. He bustled up the aisle to greet the person who had entered. He got to the front and found no one. He checked around the front displays then figured the customer had diverted to a side aisle of the store.

"Not a thoul wath there!" Viktor declared

When Viktor returned to his desk, the cash bag that he had hastily slipped in the top drawer was gone. The entire proceeds of the previous day's business evaporated along with the ghost of El Gato.

"Not a thoul wath there!" Viktor declared. He frantically grabbed his inhaler . . . squeezed and gasped . . . squeezed and gasped.

We obviously needed to adopt a more secure manner of counting our cash.

* * *

Other transgressions against Chandler Stationers tended to be botched affairs that created more mayhem than lasting damage – offenses done by rank amateurs or drunken fools. I suppose, in the long run they took their toll. Our indiscriminate alarm system was not able to distinguish revelers from Luigi's Tavern as they left for the night from real break-and-enter occurrences. A one a.m. call from the Chandler Police would draw Jeff from bed. He pulled his Levis over his pajamas and drove to Chandler to check out the situation. It was usually a false alarm. However, on a couple of occasions we had genuine night-time break-ins.

One night burglars entered the store from the roof and slipped in through the duct system. They had to be rather slight individuals to perform such a feat. They knocked over a display of cork boards as they dropped from the overhead duct to a counter and then to the floor below.

The object of the theft seemed to be a display rack of colorful bandanas – stunning, eye-catching cotton scarves. Crafters bought them to create attractive bead-studded neckwear. School kids liked them, too. But, apparently gang members tied bandanas around their heads emulating skullcaps. The perpetrators pushed the rack of kerchiefs to the door, and then realized that once inside the store they needed a key to get out.

They used the rack to break the glass in the door. And at that moment the alarm went off. The break in the glass was not large enough for escape, so the hooligans hastily renegotiated the duct system, leaving a toppled rack and a trail of bandanas behind.

They did take time to stuff their pockets with bottles of Liquid Paper. The innocuous typewriter correction fluid that came in an assortment of colors to match standard hues of copy paper contained chemicals that, when sniffed, produced a cheap high. Other possible effects from inhaling Liquid Paper included slurred speech, lack of coordination, blurred vision, nose bleeds, headaches, and hallucinations – a dreary compromise for a moment of euphoria.

Like closing the barn door after the horse got out, Jeff had metal bars welded over the duct system on the roof.

* * *

Another time we were roused from sleep by the Chandler Police. The front door to Chandler Stationers had been broken. Sure enough, when we arrived at the store at two a.m. glass shards littered the doorway and fierce daggers of ragged glass rimmed the door. The object of destruction was a heavy metal cap off of a fire hydrant that we found part way down the center aisle of the store.

In this case, the perpetrator entered the store through the hazardous opening that he had created. He proceeded to cut himself in the process. A trail of blood mapped his journey through the store.

He staggered behind the cash register which he found standing open and empty, just as we had left it the night before. He stopped at a tape display and tore into a roll of masking tape using it to staunch the flow of blood from his injury. He wandered to the back of the store and into the office. His bloody hand prints smeared the locked filing cabinet where we actually kept our money for the night, but he had not tried to force the lock. He opened the refrigerator in the stock room and helped himself to a coke, then tossed the empty can on the floor.

Drops of blood led back into the show room; they wove down another aisle and finally back out the shattered door.

Nothing of value was taken. There was the messiness of cleaning up and sterilizing a bloody trail. The greatest inconvenience and cost was replacing the glass in the door and relettering the gold-leaf script that identified the store.

For the next week I was on the lookout for a culprit swathed in gauze covering cuts he obtained during his unorthodox entry.

* * *

One day I actually chased a shoplifter down the street. Two young men had entered the store. They chose a moment when clerks were busy and several people stood at the cash register. After they came in the door they immediately parted ways and took different aisles through the store. One of the fellows carried a large paper bag, one that the Salvation Army Store around the corner packed its merchandise in. The bag looked as if it might have contained a few items from the thrift store. The two reconnoitered along the south wall and we began to hear a peculiar crunching and rustling. One fellow, the empty-handed one, suddenly headed purposefully toward the door. His partner scrambled along behind him, the paper bag clasped tightly against his chest.

"Thuthan, that guy has thomething in the thack!" Viktor screeched.

The door swung closed and the two men headed south down the block.

A wave of cold fury washed over me. *These hoodlums think they can help themselves to merchandise on the shelves and walk out the door . . .*

With more guts than good sense I dropped the greeting cards that I was about to ring up for Mrs. Kerr and bolted through the door like a scalded cat. The guy carrying the paper bag was somewhat encumbered by its bulkiness and weight. I caught up with him in front of the bootery and tapped him on the shoulder. He spun around, shoved the bag at me, and took off after his fleet-footed friend.

The item in the bag, loosely covered by a lady's sweater and a tablecloth from the thrift store, was one of our most expensive postal scales, a heavy-duty platform scale that weighed parcels up to twenty-five pounds.

If these guys were weighing marijuana they were

doing it in industrial-size packages!

* * *

A woman was looking with interest at a display of lead crystal that was in the front window. I did not recognize her as one of our regular customers. Perhaps a tourist. Perhaps a guest at the San Marcos Hotel. She wore smartly creased blue linen slacks and a coordinated jacket. Her hair was neatly coiffed, though a bit brassy in my estimation. She obviously had some appreciation of lead crystal. I showed the pieces to her one by one – a slender bud vase, a pair of pillar candlesticks, a celery dish.

"I'd like to see that fruit bowl," she said.

I carefully extracted a heavy bowl from the back of the shelf and handed it to her.

She fingered the sharply incised starburst patterns on the piece knowingly. Crystal facets winked and reflected the lights above the counter.

The lady had in her hands a parcel from another store. "Will you give me one of your bags?" She asked me. "This one is about to break."

I retrieved a sack from under the cash register. The lady slipped her flimsy bag into the more substantial bag I presented.

She thanked me and added, "I'll have to think about the crystal."

It took her about ten seconds to think. Within a minute the woman was gone. And so was the crystal fruit bowl. It went out of the store in a Chandler Stationers merchandise bag that I had generously provided.

Chapter 24

DEATH ROW

What I knew about the Arizona Prison system I read in the newspaper or in regional history books.

The Arizona State Prison was constructed in Florence in the early 1900s to replace the notorious territorial prison in Yuma. Convicts living in tents built the new prison. One of the key features of the facility was the death chamber. Scaffolding above death row cells had a trap door. A condemned prisoner was tethered by the neck, the trap door fell open, and the body dropped into a room below. Death could be instantaneous; however, gory results such as decapitation or slow asphyxiation were also possible. Execution by hanging was the mode of the day. Twenty-eight inmates of the Arizona State Prison were executed in this manner.

In 1933 the gas chamber was installed. Poison gas was pumped into a room while the prisoner slept. More humane? The individuals involved couldn't tell. Thirty-eight executions were carried out in this manner.

In 1992 lethal injection was adopted. A prisoner was strapped onto a gurney and a needle was inserted into his veins. The chemicals dispensed put him to sleep and hopefully reduced muscle spasms. Twenty or so executions by lethal injection had been performed.

The knowledge I had of this chamber of horrors was tenuous at best. However, several prison relationships were established in the years that we had the store.

* * *

My first experience dealing with prison protocol occurred after a nice woman made some purchases. She bought a simple writing tablet, a package of envelopes, and an assortment of pens. She also selected a large padded envelope. She removed the smaller envelopes from their packaging and dropped them loosely into the larger padded envelope. She added the tablet and the pens.

"These are going to an acquaintance in the state prison in Florence," she said. "I'd like to include these, too." She dropped a small booklet of stamps in the parcel.

"The prison requires that packages to inmates be packed by an established business," she continued. "And an official business receipt must be enclosed."

I complied with her request. I addressed the larger envelope with the information she gave me – the inmate's name, serial number and cell block – and added the store's return address label to the pack. I enclosed a proper receipt and sealed the envelope.

"I need for this to go out this afternoon," my new customer said. "I will take it to the post office myself."

The nice lady thanked me and walked out the door with the parcel. Time passed. I thought no more about the transaction. One afternoon I received a telephone call from the Arizona State Prison. The warden asked me about a certain parcel sent to inmate #92378.

"What was in the package?"

My mind snapped into rewind. All I could remember about the package was the envelopes, the tablet, and the pens. Oh, yes. The little booklet of stamps.

"Who made the purchase?"

"I didn't know the lady."

"Did you address the package?"

"Yes."

"Did you seal the package?"

"Yes."

"Did you mail the package?"

Here he had me. I had not mailed the package.

The warden thanked me for the information and the conversation was over.

A few days later I received a yellow card from the Department of Corrections, Arizona State Prison, Florence. It concerned the parcel sent to inmate #92378. "Delivery Denied" in imposing letters across the top of the card. "Contraband Enclosed" checked as reason for denial.

My gosh! What had been added to that innocuous envelope?

Henceforth I carefully documented the items and the purchasers of any product I sent to the state prison.

* * *

When another inmate began a correspondence with the store I was far more cautious. Neatly scripted on lined notebook paper:

Dear Sir or Madam,

My name is Javier Hernandez. I am an inmate in the Arizona State Prison in Florence. Please to send me information about the following art supplies. How much is each?

> *Sketch pad, 9x12, 70# paper, (Bienfang, if possible)*
> *Prismacolor Art Stix, set of 8 (What is the cost of a set of 12?)*
> *Sable watercolor brush #4*
> *Sable watercolor brush #10*
> *Layout pencil*
> *Small kneaded eraser*

What is cost of postage for this order?

Sincerely,
Javier Hernandez
Inmate #98835
Arizona State Prison
Florence, Ariz.

Javier obviously knew his art supplies. It turned out that several levels of communication transpired before I could fill his order.

Dear Javier Hernandez,
Concerning your inquiry about art supplies:

Strathmore Sketch pad, 9x12, 70# paper	*7.59*
(We do not carry Bienfang)	
Prismacolor Art Stix, set of 12	*10.99*
(We only have set of 12 in stock)	
Sable watercolor brush #4	*6.99*
Sable watercolor brush #10	*15.99*
Layout pencil	*.69*
Small kneaded eraser	*.49*

Sincerely,
Chandler Stationers

Dear Sir or Madam,
I cannot buy the watercolor brushes at this time. Too expensive. I will purchase the other items. Please to send bill.
Sincerely,
Javier Hernandez
Inmate #98835
Arizona State Prison
Florence, Ariz.

INVOICE
CHANDLER STATIONERS
Javier Hernandez
Inmate #98835
Arizona State Prison

Strathmore Sketch pad, 9x12, 70# paper	*7.59*
Prismacolor Art Stix, set of 12	*10.99*
Layout pencil	*.69*

Small kneaded eraser .49
Sub total 19.76
Tax .98
Shipping & Handling 1.50
Total 22.24

MONEY ORDER
Pay to the order of CHANDLER STATIONERS $22.24
Twenty two & 24/100
Javier Hernandez

I carefully packaged the art supplies. I enclosed an invoice stamped *Paid in Full* then sealed the parcel. I carried it to the post office and personally handed it to a clerk who affixed the proper postage before my eyes. This package passed inspection.

From time-to-time during his incarceration, Javier ordered art supplies from Chandler Stationers. The same convoluted correspondence accompanied each order. I couldn't help but cheer the man on. I hoped, if he were released from prison, that he made a go of his interest in art.

* * *

Another loose connection I established with the Arizona State Prison occurred when a rangy cowboy drifted into the store. He flashed an I.D. card that indicated he had come on the business of the Arizona State Prison.

"Ma'am," he drawled. "There's going to be a rodeo in this state like none you have ever seen."

"Oh?"

"An Outlaw Rodeo it is."

"An outlaw rodeo?"

"There's going to be a rodeo at the Arizona State Prison in Florence. Inmates convicted of charges such as murder, aggravated burglary, and narcotics will participate in events like barrel racing, bronc riding, team roping, and chute dogging."

Naturally I was curious.

"Not only that," he continued. "There will be events like Wild-Cow Milking. A team of inmates tries to subdue a Black Angus long enough to extract some milk.

"Or Convict Poker. Four inmates sit around a table in the middle of the rodeo arena playing a friendly game of poker. A wild bull is released with the sole purpose of unseating the poker players. Last man to leave his seat is the winner.

"And then there is Bust Out. Six angry bulls roar out of their chutes bearing temporarily attached cowboys who are wearing prison stripes. Last man to remain on his bull wins the event."

By now he had me chuckling. "How do these convicts get to participate in such a rodeo?"

"Some of them were ranch hands and had rodeo experience, but any convict who has guts and a clean prison record can try out."

"When is this amazing event?" I asked.

"March 15th and 16th," he replied. "And you can help the production by buying an ad in the Outlaw Rodeo Program."

How could I say no? I placed a small ad in the program.

* * *

One little lady bustled in the door near closing time. She brought a sheaf of papers and proceeded to the Xerox machine. From then on we saw her rather regularly, always near closing time. She never purchased anything, but she made copies by the ream. We exchanged pleasantries. I eventually learned that she was a volunteer at the Arizona State Prison.

"I am a reading tutor," she told me. "Every Thursday afternoon I work with inmates who are not good readers."

Wow! What an unusual commitment! My volunteer activities centered on a Girl Scout Troop and a fifth grade Sunday school class.

"Other volunteers offer their time as counselors,

mentors, spiritual advocates, and recreation leaders," she added.

During this time newspaper stories about an impending execution at the Arizona State Prison hit the fan. Diego Diaz (not his name) had been convicted of a list of heinous atrocities. First-degree murder, armed robbery, aggravated assault, concealing criminal property. Diego had killed a woman in a botched convenience-store robbery and subsequent carjacking. He had been sitting on death-row for ten years. His appeals had run out, and the execution was scheduled. Much controversy surrounded this particular execution. But, I suppose controversy surrounds any execution.

The little lady bearing sheaves came in more frequently. The copy machine spit out more volumes of the printed page. Whatever our little customer was doing, she was doing in great magnitude.

We came to learn that she had been preparing letters, documents, and pleas for leniency toward Diego Diaz.

"Please take this," she said and handed me a page from her stack of copies. It contained a synopsis of some of the common arguments opposing the death penalty.

- *There is no way to remedy the occasional mistake.*
- *Race and place determine who lives and who dies.*
- *We pay millions for the death penalty system.*
- *Poor quality defense leaves many sentenced to death.*
- *There are strong religious reasons to oppose the death penalty*
- *Even the condemned deserve to live.*
- *There is a better alternative: life without parole.*

The story did not have a happy ending. A committee of protesters staged a candle-light vigil outside the prison gates at Florence. The governor did not issue a stay-of-execution. The death sentence went off as scheduled – lethal injection, the mode of execution of the day.

The clincher came a few weeks later. The little lady was back in the store. She had but two pages to copy this time.

"Thank you for the courtesies you extended to me these past months," she said. "I felt comfortable bringing my project into this store. You were kind."

I was at a loss for words knowing that her efforts on behalf of Diego Diaz had failed. "I'm glad you came in," was all I could say.

And then she told me, "I am the widow of Diego Diaz. I married Diego while he was on death row."

Was justice served?

Chapter 25

MEN OF THE CLOTH

My notary service was a nice sideline to the do-it-yourself legal forms that we sold. Rather frequently I was asked to notarize a Quit Claim Deed, a Power of Attorney, or a Declaration of Homestead. As well as occasional court documents I also notarized vehicle transfer forms for people who were selling their cars.

I teetered at the top of a tall ladder rearranging a row of storage boxes on an upper shelf. A man blustered through the door.

"Where's your notary?" he demanded as he advanced to the counter and began signing a stack of documents that he pulled from a manila folder.

It took me a few minutes to unload my burden, negotiate the ladder, and get over to the counter. By then the papers were signed.

"Sir, you should not have signed these until I could personally witness them," I commented.

"My dear girl." *He called me my-dear-girl!* "You know that I signed these! Here is my I.D." And he handed me a driver's license from Ohio. *Fr. Stephan Reasbeck, M. Div.*

What was this M. Div.? A religious designation, no doubt. Master of Divinity?

The visage before me certainly looked like the picture on the driver's license. As in the picture, he was wearing a black clergy shirt that had a neat white neckband. Thinning grey hair plastered over a receding hair line. Horn rimmed glasses perched on a sharp beak of a nose. And, yes, the camera caught a subtle sneer between his nose and his upper lip. Closer scrutiny of the man himself revealed that he was wearing black pants and shiny black shoes. He certainly looked the part of a distinguished priest. But, that's where the similarity stopped.

Father Stephan, as he wanted me to call him, became a thorn in my side. Having found a convenient notary public, he came to the store at frequent intervals demanding notary signatures on various court documents that he carried in his portfolio.

Fr. Stephan Reasbeck, M. Div. had his fingers in numerous law suits in the small claims court of Maricopa County and pursued them with vengeance. A branch from his neighbor's eucalyptus tree fell during a summer store. It smashed a line of rose bushes that Father Stephan had planted earlier in the spring. He sought damages. Father Stephan took his cat to the vet, and the cat died. He declared medical malpractice against the unsuspecting animal surgeon. A local auto mechanic put a rebuilt carburetor in Father Stephan's car, and the car stalled in the middle of Arizona Avenue. Father Stephan maintained negligence and shoddy workmanship. Working things out amicably did not seem to be part of the picture. Father Stephan sought retribution through the small claims courts in Arizona.

"Huh," snorted Viktor who attended St. Mary's Church. "If he'th a Catholic pwietht, he ith a defwocked pwietht."

I simply notarized his documents, logged them in my record book, and got Father Stephan out the door as quickly as possible. I figured if he stubbed a toe in Chandler Stationers we would be the next recipient of a Summons to Court.

Father Stephan was the exception. Other men of the cloth who graced our establishment were devout servants of God.

* * *

Most of the local churches had charge accounts at Chandler Stationers. Ministers and secretaries stopped in to purchase paper and ink, pens and paper clips and other accoutrements to running a church office. We offered a small discount to the churches as a way of showing our appreciation for their business.

Brother Jeremiah shuffled in one afternoon. His faded bib overalls had fresh mud spots on the knees which was testament to his part-time day job, working in Mrs. Chamberlain's garden. His week-end job and the passion of his life was his role as pastor of the Spirit of Joy Pentecostal congregation south of town. The little white clapboard church on a side street off of Arizona Avenue had seen better days. Paint peeled from its scarred walls. Roof shingles curled, and tin coffee can lids were tacked over spots where shingles were missing.

Brother Jeremiah's hair was curly and white like sheep's wool. His face was as black as ink. Because some of his teeth were missing his chin almost touched his nose. Brother Jeremiah had brought the Word of God to his flock for upwards of forty years.

Brother Jeremiah wanted to look at our briefcases. "It would be so nice to tote my Bible, my devotion books, and my congregation list in a briefcase," he said. "Right now I use paper bags." He lifted a wrinkled and splitting Bashas' grocery bag in his right hand.

Jeff led Brother Jeremiah to a row of portfolios and attaché cases. Numerous styles were available. Some were leather; some were constructed of Tufide which was a durable synthetic fabric. Various choices in style included brass or nickel plated hardware, one or two divided pockets, key or combination lock. What caught Brother Jeremiah's eye was a premium leather case. Euro style, soft rounded edges, tailored beige interior. The cost, seventy-five dollars.

"Oh my," cackled Brother Jeremiah. "That's too

much briefcase for this ole jack-leg preacher."

"Well . . . what was your budget?" Jeff hedged.

"I had in mind I might spend twenty dollars. Even that was robbin' Peter to pay Paul."

The most economical of our cases in those days cost a good deal more than twenty dollars.

Jeff didn't miss a beat. "You know, we were about to reduce the price on this briefcase. I'll check, but I believe we were going to reduce it to twenty dollars. With your church discount it would be eighteen.

Brother Jeremiah left the store with a handsome new briefcase to carry on his rounds as he ministered to his congregation.

* * *

A distinguished gentleman came into my life one balmy spring afternoon. He was withered and frail, but his genteel manner and polite speech identified him as a man of culture. He spoke with a slight European accent which added to his air of distinction. A Roman collar at the throat of a short-sleeved clergy shirt identified him as a priest.

A younger man had accompanied him into the store. "Dad, they have Esterbrook pen points. Come over here," I overheard the younger man say.

Dad? I was mildly surprised. I had pegged the customer as a Catholic priest. But, of course, Protestant pastors occasionally wore clerical collars. It was just not common in Chandler.

The two men conferred for a moment. The elder decided to purchase an extra fine flexible nib for his pen. "These are getting hard to find," he said. He seemed pleased with his purchase.

Dom Hubrecht Schuyler was a newcomer to Chandler and had moved into one of the assisted living/independent living facilities that had sprung up in the East Valley. He seemed anxious to acquaint himself with the area.

From then on he paid frequent visits to the stationers, purchasing small items like note pads and fountain pen ink.

I enjoyed visiting with Dom Schuyuler and, in time, learned that he was a recently ordained Benedictine Priest. He had immigrated to the United States from the Netherlands after World War II. His wife had died in recent years. He had a large family, children who were probably about my age. It was his oldest son who had accompanied him to our store on his first visit. Until then I did not know that a man who had been married and had raised a family could become a Catholic priest.

"When I was a young man I intended to become a Jesuit," Dom Schuyler told me. "But World War II came along and my life changed."

I listened with rapt attention as he told me he had been caught up in the Dutch Resistance when the Nazis invaded the Netherlands in the early years of the war.

Following The War he had had a long and happy marriage and a successful family. He was now a widower and planned to end his years as a Benedictine priest.

One day Dom Schuyler timidly presented me with a book he had written.

"You might like to read this," he said. He had inscribed the inside flyleaf to me.

The Resistance was an account of his underground activities against the Nazis. In the course of The War Hubrecht Schuyler was imprisoned, tortured, and sentenced to death. He wrote of his ordeals with unyielding devotion to God and Country and even managed to spice up the harrowing narrative with bits of humor.

I ferreted out that Hubrecht Schuyler had been awarded the coveted Dutch War Cross as well as Belgian's Highest Cross of Honor for his valor. This innocuous Benedictine Priest had been a true hero of World War II. He was living out his days with memories of his valiant exploits and sharing them with a sympathetic shop girl.

* * *

Pastor Leonard Erickson was minister of the North Side Baptist Church. His prosperous congregation had just completed a new sanctuary. We had followed the construction of the sanctuary, and we knew that Pastor Erickson was pleased with this edifice built to the glory of God. Pastor Erickson and his wife, an amiable couple, had come to the store to purchase supplies for the newly decorated church office.

Halloween was around the corner. We had unpacked orange and black plates, napkins and crepe paper streamers. Cardboard pumpkins, witches, and cats were strewn in the aisles. We sorted through the stock and decided we did not need as much as we had. I filled two boxes with mismatched and slightly shelf-worn Halloween décor, carry-over from previous years. When the director of the Boys and Girls Club came in I gave him a box of Halloween party ware to decorate the club house. He was pleased with the donation.

Here was Pastor Erickson. Maybe the Baptist youth group could use the other box.

"Oh no!" Pastor Erickson puffed up like an indignant toad. "Halloween is a day of the devil. We do not acknowledge the devil in our church. You are promoting Satan when you sell such things in your store."

Dear me! I was skating on thin theological ice.

I gave the decorations to the Presbyterians.

Chapter 26

DIAMONDS ARE A GIRL'S BEST FRIEND

She might have retired five years earlier for she had been drawing modest Social Security checks since she was sixty-two years old. The fact was that Lillian had to work. She juggled mortgage and credit card payments with a catalog of other expenses that went with general living. No savings, no investments, no pension to keep her afloat in what should have been a period of active retirement.

Lillian lived in a condominium complex that was running to seed. She had been one of the first residents to take out a mortgage in the Town and Country Villas. She envisioned resort-style living — manicured lawns, a club-house open to residents of the villa, a spa and sauna, and mini gym. The villa swimming pool was right under her second floor window and Lillian anticipated swimming a few leisurely laps every evening.

For a while Lillian enjoyed the amenities offered by the villa, but before long things began to go south. The developer of Town and Country Villas had not been able to sell all of the units to resident owners. The many vacant units were sold at reduced prices to investors who turned them into time-share apartments. Lillian was surrounded by vacationers who had raucous parties, splashed in the pool all night, and then draped soggy towels over the balconies and banisters of the complex. They did not have the pride of home ownership. Through the night doors slammed, pipes rattled, toilets flushed, and floorboards shook.

Week after week it was the same. One set of revelers moved out and another set moved in. Selling her small niche of Town and Country Villas under these deteriorating conditions was not economically feasible.

Life had not always been penurious for Lillian. She had been divorced from Roger for over twenty years. Whether it was part of the divorce settlement or whether it was largesse on the part of Roger, Lillian walked away from the marriage with a beautiful diamond ring and a small monthly stipend. She had only herself to take care of. Her three children were young adults at the time of the divorce and had dispersed over the country. Lillian moved to Chandler and got a job at a new jewelry store on the north end of town. She sold luxury baubles and fine watches. Although her own reduced circumstances did not allow her to indulge in jeweled extravagances, she enjoyed the elegance vicariously. Plus, she had her own gorgeous diamond to flit before the eyes of serious jewelry buyers.

Unfortunately, Gershwin's Galleria was not long-lived. It hobbled into receivership and Lillian lost her job along with several weeks of back-salary. When she came to work for us she might not have known anything about expanding files or typewriter ribbons but she did know about gemstones and diamonds.

And then Roger died. And so did the monthly checks that cushioned the financial impact of medical expenses, insurance premiums, homeowner fees, utilities, and car maintenance. Lillian ran a tight, but sinking, ship. A chicken purchased after church at the grocer's deli provided suppers for a week. By the end of the month she did not have two nickels to rub together. Her car was old. Her wardrobe was threadbare. Her shoe leather was thin. That was life. She got by.

* * *

Marieta Enos grew up on the Gila River Indian Reservation south of Chandler. Her original family home was a one-room hovel of wattle and daub construction. It hunkered under the desert sun, at one with the environment, unencumbered by neighbors and noise and the impediments of society. As a child, Marieta toiled in the long rows of her family's irrigated garden where corn, muskmelon, and squash provided staples of their diet. She watched her grandmother grind corn on worn stone metates. She helped to harvest sticky red fruit from the tops of giant saguaro cactus with long spliced poles crafted for that purpose. She sat beside her mother and grandmother as they split willow twigs that would be woven into magnificent baskets.

Before Marieta could hone her skills as a traditional Pima maiden, she was sent to Phoenix Indian School to learn the ways of white people. Upon graduation from Indian School she returned to the reservation to marry Woodrow.

She lived in a reservation neighborhood of BIA subsidized homes. Three rows of modular houses were laid out across the desert floor like Lego blocks. The ready-to-assemble homes had been brought onto the reservation to provide modern conveniences for the Indians. They soon lost their new-home sheen. The walls were thin; the pipes rattled; the floorboards shook. Half-naked children scampered about the dusty yards. Mangy curs scratched sandy burrows in the fragile desert shade. Disabled vehicles studded the yards, some mounted on cinder blocks, others sunk dismally into the sand on rotten and splayed tires. Towels, blue jeans, and BVD's flapped on higgledy-piggledy clothes lines.

Marieta's life had always been one of penny-pinching frugality. She had been a widow for the past twelve years. Woodrow had died of complications related to diabetes, a disease attributed to lifestyle and dietary changes in the Indian community. Pensions and insurance were unheard of. Her sons left the reservation. Two daughters and their burgeoning families continued to live nearby. Marieta was surrounded by six grandchildren plus assorted aunts, uncles, nieces, nephews, in-laws and out-laws who ran at will in and out the doors of the modular homes of the neighborhood.

Marieta scraped along as best she could with tribal

entitlements. Her car was old. Her dress was faded. Her shoes were cracked. She missed Woodrow, but her life was full. She got by.

* * *

A person will never feel completely down-and-out if he has one item of value, whether it is of intrinsic appeal or of significant worldly worth. And Lillian had one such item. When she walked out of her marriage she kept the ring that symbolized her betrothal to Roger. A brilliant diamond sparkled on her finger; an elongated shape, the luminous stone tapered to a point at each end. Lillian was proud of that ring. Its very elegance linked her to a finer time. Although she had transferred it to the third finger of her right hand so that it wouldn't be interpreted as an engagement ring, she flashed it as conspicuously as any young fiancée. Lillian knew diamonds and flushed with pleasure when her majestic gem was noticed.

Marieta Enos came into the store late in the day. She often lingered at the card racks. Family was important to Marieta. Any month of the year she had a list of relatives for whom to buy birthday cards, anniversary cards, and get well cards. Marieta approached the cash register with cards she had selected for upcoming events in the life of the Enos family.

Lillian reached for Marieta's cards to ring up the transaction. The stone on her right finger twinkled alluringly.

"Your diamond!" Marieta gasped. "May I see?"

Lillian's outstretched hand paused over the greeting cards stacked on the counter.

Marieta scrambled among crumpled tissues, gasoline receipts, pencil stubs, shopping lists, and loose change rattling about in her cavernous black purse. Momentarily she produced a jeweler's loupe, and with expert concentration brought the small magnifying device to her right eye. She drew Lillian's outstretched hand under its 10X magnification.

"Ah, a Marquis Brilliant Cut diamond," Marieta exclaimed. "Yours is particularly radiant. Is this an old family jewel?"

"Why, I have had this ring for nearly fifty years," Lillian replied. "It was my engagement ring." She proceeded to go into detail about how she had left the husband but kept the ring.

"Because the Marquis diamond tapers to a point at both extremities, it is very difficult to cut," Marieta continued. "The sharp points are fragile."

"Most brides choose the round brilliant diamond," Lillian contributed. "But I selected the Marquis because I thought it was more flattering to my hand." Lillian slipped the ring off of her finger and handed it to Marieta.

Marieta studied the stone in closer detail. "The round brilliant diamond has set the standard for all other diamond shapes. It has fifty-eight facets that maximize fire and brilliance," she said.

"Yes," said Lillian. "The Marquis typically has fifty-six facets. It compares favorably to the round brilliant."

"*Carat, cut, color*, and *clarity* are the four C's that determine the beauty of a diamond," Marieta said. "But *cut* is considered the most important. A well-cut diamond can appear to be of greater carat weight than it actually is. Your stone was cut by an experienced diamond cutter."

* * *

This unlikely conversation between a shop-girl and a Pima Indian woman could only have taken place in Chandler, Arizona. In the early 1960's Harry Winston, internationally known jeweler, established a diamond processing plant near the Gila River Indian Reservation. They sought skilled Indian people who had worked with jewelry. Tribal members who passed a stringent security test were hired and trained as diamond cutters. The diamond plant was a significant source of employment for Pima Indians who lived on the reservation. Each morning they were bussed from the reservation to work at the plant and bussed home again at night. Marieta Enos was one of the diamond cutters.

Two women, culturally separate, yet circumstantially alike, found a common denominator in a gemstone of ancient appeal, mystical power, and of intrinsic beauty.

Chapter 27

DEAD OR ALIVE

"Chandler Stationers. May I help you?" I reached for a note pad near the telephone.

"Who?" My pen was poised to begin writing.

"I'm sorry." I frowned. "I didn't understand your name."

"Bonjo?" I tenuously repeated what I had heard.

"What can I do for you Mr. Bonjo?"

"Lady . . . I . . . am . . . Bon Jovi," the caller proclaimed.

A pregnant silence.

"Oh?"

"Jon . . . Bon Jovi," he clarified.

"I see."

"My band is playing at Wild Horse Pass."

"Indeed?"

"We had a concert last night."

"How nice."

". . . and we'll have another tonight."

"My goodness."

"We need some finger counters."

"Do you mean tally counters?"

"Yes. We need to keep a gate count."

"We should have finger tally counters."

"I need six."

"Let me see what we have."

I put the caller on hold while I went to the cabinet

where we kept such devices.

A tally counter was a mechanical apparatus used for incrementally counting people or things. They were used for tallying inventories, for counting traffic in stores, or for recording attendance at events. An usher standing at a door or gate could press the button on this finger-held gadget each time a person went through and record how many people entered an area. Each little contraption could register a count of up to 9999. With six counters this guy could keep track of an audience of almost 60,000 people. Wow. That was more than the population of Chandler.

"Jeff." I encountered my husband in the center aisle. "Some guy named Bon Jovi needs six tally counters"

"We should have tally counters in the front cabinet," Jeff said.

"He says he is giving a concert at Wild Horse Pass. Do you know who he is?"

Jeff shrugged his shoulders. "Dunno."

"Bon Jovi!" shrieked daughter Katie. She was working at the store for the summer. "Mom! Dad! I can't believe you don't know who Bon Jovi is! His newest album is *Slippery When Wet*."

"Well . . . wet or dry . . . that bit of musical trivia slipped by me."

"The smash hit on that album, 'Wanted Dead or Alive,' is simply . . . to die for!" Katie was ecstatic.

I didn't like her analogy.

"Oh . . . well . . . he's performing at Wild Horse Pass tonight."

Wild Horse Pass was a new luxury hotel and Las Vegas-style casino built on the Gila River Indian Reservation. They were getting a reputation for attracting major entertainers.

"I'd give *anything* to go to his concert! . . . Maybe you could take me and Tracy tonight?"

I looked at my fifteen-year-old daughter over the top of my spectacles. There was no way I would drive out to

Wild Horse Pass for an evening concert. And she couldn't drive herself.

"I guess not, huh?" Katie interpreted my non-response without my having to say a word.

Ah, we had twelve tally counters in the drawer. We hadn't sold any since our last order. We could, indeed, fill Bon Jovi's order of six. I returned to the phone.

"Yes, we can supply six tally counters. They are $13.95 each."

"Deliver them to the San Marcos Hotel. Room 285. ASAP." The phone slammed in my ear.

"Ab . . . so . . . lutely . . ." I found myself talking to a dial tone.

I invoiced the six counters, put them in a sack, and set the parcel beside the cash register for Jeff to deliver to the San Marcos Hotel. Nice little sale, even if the customer was quite abrupt.

When Jeff finished his task at hand he went to the register to get the parcel.

"Where are those finger counters?"

"Beside the register."

"I don't see them."

"Humpf." *That man couldn't see a carrot if it was tied on his nose.*

I bustled up to the counter to retrieve the conspicuous package. There could be no mistaking its contents or its destination. The invoice was stapled to the outside of the bag.

"Right here beside . . ." I paused in mid-sentence.

The package containing the finger counters was not where I had put it.

I queried Lillian.

"No, I didn't see the package."

"I left it right here," I insisted.

I queried Viktor.

"I thaw you put a thack on the counter. I'm thowwy. I don't know where it ith now."

"Katie, do you know . . .?" but Katie had retreated to

the back room and was not within earshot.

"Not fifteen minutes ago. I left it right here!" I banged the counter with my fist, and then tore into the drawers under the cash register. An intensive search of the check-out station did not reveal the whereabouts of the elusive sack full of finger counters.

Slippery When Wet. These contraptions were apparently slippery when dry.

Had Bon Jovi or a cohort been waiting in the wings ready to grab the merchandise as soon as it was put out for them? The idea was preposterous.

Had a customer inadvertently picked up the sack along with his merchandise? He would probably bring it back.

Had it been the object of shoplifting? Not a hot shoplifting target.

Meanwhile an impatient customer was waiting at the hotel for his finger counters.

I returned to the cabinet and pulled out the remaining six counters, invoiced them to Bon Jovi, San Marcos Hotel, Room 285. They left my hands only when I turned the package over to Jeff who immediately walked it to the hotel which was a block north of the store.

"Katie!" Jeff roared when he returned from his mission.

A terrified head poked out of the stockroom door.

"What possessed you?"

Katie shuffled up the aisle. "Well . . . someone had to make that delivery. I thought it might as well be me."

"You . . . didn't . . . know . . ." Jeff spoke each word forcefully and deliberately. ". . .*what* . . . you might run into." He could barely contain his rage over his daughter tripping off to a rock star's hotel room.

"I know, Dad." Katie appeared properly chastised. "A guy wearing a shoulder holster came to the door. That scared me plenty."

"Yes . . . he came to the door when I arrived, too."

"Mom. . ." Katie interrupted her dad's tirade. "Bon Jovi has more money than God. I could see into that room. Piles of money. Loose bills. Heaps of coins. On the beds, on the tables, on the floor. . .

"But, here," Katie added as if in penance, "is payment for the six finger counters." She gave me a handful of cash.

"And here," contributed Jeff, "is payment for the other six counters."

"Oh, my!" I said. "We'll have to refund one of those payments."

"No," Jeff continued, "When the guy sporting the gun holster answered the door, he told me that a girl had just delivered some finger counters. Then he shrugged his shoulders and said they'd keep these, too."

"Was that Bon Jovi?"

"I couldn't pick Bon Jovi out of a paper bag if he were the only item in it," answered Jeff.

"I don't think it was," said Katie. Then she added, "There were a couple of other men in the room sifting through money and running tabulations on calculators. Maybe one of them was Bon Jovi."

"Do you suppose they were counting the proceeds from last night's concert?" I asked.

"Who knows?" Jeff replied. "If so, it looked as if the revenues from the concert had been thrown into a big cauldron and were just now being sorted out.

"You'd think there would be a more systematic way to deal with concert tickets." I shook my head, perplexed.

Katie didn't press to attend the Bon Jovi concert. Her experience at the hotel seemed to dampen her enthusiasm for that night's performance. Guns and money put a spin of fear and intrigue into the mix. Besides, she hadn't even seen the famous rock star.

That night I heard a thumping and thudding behind Katie's closed bedroom door. "Wanted . . ." occasionally drifted above the cacophony. ". . .dead or alive . . ."

Wanted Dead or Alive. The mystery of the fugitive finger totes had been solved.

Chapter 28

GONE WITH THE WIND

Twenty minutes after six and I finally locked the door behind Mr. Ridenour. He was three sheets to the wind when he stumbled into the store at closing time on Christmas Eve. He had come from the direction of Luigi's Tavern and an aura of stale beer and cigarette smoke followed him into the store.

Outside, the Tumbleweed Christmas tree stood sentinel in the lonely park. Chandler's unique contribution to holiday ornamentation was a mound of two-thousand tumbleweeds corralled into a wire frame structure resembling a giant Christmas tree. The renegade weeds were sprayed with white paint and fire retardant. Twelve-hundred blinking winking lights had lured the population of Chandler to the town square for the past month. The pre-holiday festivities were past. Choristers were gone. Santa's house was empty. Not a soul was in the park.

"A bit of last minute shopping," Mr. Ridenour explained sheepishly. He pulled his felt fedora off his head and twisted the brim anxiously. His hair was mussed and two errant tufts stuck out over his ears. "I need something nice for the Missus."

Mr. Ridenour actually looked a bit like the man of the season. In his staid and sober insurance persona, Mr. Ridenour sported a neatly trimmed white goatee to complement his thick rug of white hair. Tonight his flushed cheeks and twinkly eyes embodied holiday cheer, the kind served up at Luigi's. A Rudolph the Red-Nosed Reindeer novelty tie was knotted askew around his neck, and Rudolph's red nose blinked deliriously.

"You old goat," I muttered silently and rolled my eyes heavenward.

My long-suffering sales clerks garnered their weary forces and made several suggestions, their eyes on the clock, with hopes of a quick sale. Something small. Something classy.

"I believe Madeleine would like a silver candy dish," suggested Dorcas. She was friends with Madeleine Ridenour through their Eastern Star affiliations.

"Or a gold Sheaffer pen and pencil set?" contributed Lillian.

"Or, perhaps a lapis lazuli inlaid jewelry box?" I added.

We had hit all the precious elements in the store. We knew Mr. Ridenour could afford them. He was a prosperous insurance broker. He shook his head obstinately at each suggestion.

"I need something really nice," he mumbled. "Really, really nice," he repeated lamely. "What about that?"

I followed his gaze to an upper shelf of the window display. He pointed to a magnificent ruby glass lamp that glowed suggestively amid bedraggled artificial holly. Somehow by Christmas Eve all of our holiday displays looked disarranged and dusty.

"Why yes," I stammered. "That is called a Gone with the Wind Lamp. It costs $350."

That lamp might have come off a parlor table in a New Orleans bordello. A rich red glow emitted from its fragile glass globes, a color both seasonal and evocative. It didn't seem like the kind of thing the dour Madeleine Ridenour would display in her front window. But then a tipsy husband didn't fit the domestic picture either.

A Gone with the Wind Lamp is an elegant version of an old fashioned hurricane lamp. It got its popular name from the movie of the same title, although, in actuality, Gone with the Wind Lamps did not emerge into Victorian parlors until ten years after the Civil War. Of course, ours was electrified, but it had the same basic parts as the historic versions. The base of a GWTW lamp has a fragile colored-glass globe that rests upon an ornate brass stand. A second and matching glass globe sits above the first, cradled by an intricate circular frame, also brass.

In the electrified lamps, a totally non-functional clear glass chimney protrudes several inches above the upper glass globe emulating the original lamps that burned oil. This particular lamp was further enhanced by a ring of prisms dangling from the filigree brass mid section. The prisms, reflecting lights from the outside colonnade, created pin points of light that winked and danced in a salacious come-hither manner over the ceiling.

"I'll take it if you can wrap it up pretty for me right away." Mr. Ridenour had made his decision.

Inwardly I groaned. Christmas Eve. It was already past closing time.

Packaging a Gone with the Wind Lamp was a three-clerk job at a minimum. Lillian negotiated a ladder and disassembled the lamp piece by piece. It was rather like dismantling the Taj Mahal – removing its marbled onion dome, its jeweled minarets, and its finials. She carefully raised the upper globe of the lamp from the tower and handed it to Dorcas who stood below securing the ladder. Lillian gently extracted the chimney, fifteen inches of sheer glass tubing held in place by brass fingers surrounding a forty-watt light bulb. That, too, was passed gingerly down to Dorcas. Then came the filigree frame with fifty dancing prisms that cast maniacal shards of light over the shelves. Finally Lillian lifted the bottom globe and its surprisingly sturdy brass base leaving in its stead a clear ring on the shelf around which a layer of Christmas dust had settled.

Meanwhile, I scurried about the attic looking for a foam lined crate that this particular lamp came in. There was a reason why we kept a mountain of empty storage boxes in the attic. One and only one box was designated for this lamp. With the right box, globes, chimneys, frames, and prisms nestled securely in pre-formed spaces. But finding the right box in a jam-packed attic was a sport much like finding the golden Easter egg. Empty boxes got shoved around as more important seasonal merchandise or over-stocked product took over.

Eventually, crate and lamp parts were united in the stock room. First we had to employ Windex to shine the lamp and each of its fifty twinkly prisms. Then we puzzled over the allotted spaces in the foam lined box. Lamp parts matched the foam indentures in one manner only. Fitting them together was like working a three-D jigsaw puzzle or lining up the numbers on a Rubik cube.

When the carton was assembled it took the three of us to piece holiday paper together to encircle a cubic yard of unwieldy package. It felt like we were gift wrapping a battleship. In honor of the grandeur of the gift I took from the shelves one of Hallmark's deluxe bows and wearily popped it atop the box.

Forty-five minutes after Mr. Ridenour had staggered into the store we hefted the bedecked parcel onto a merchandise cart, and I rolled it out to the only vehicle left on the town square. I watched with bated breath as Mr. Ridenour transferred it into the trunk of his Lincoln Town Car.

"Oh Christmas tree, Oh Christmas tree," a clear melody rang through the crisp night air. The city had rigged up musical accompaniment for the lone Christmas tree. The refrain morphed into "God Rest Ye Merry Gentlemen" as Mr. Ridenour began a carefully calculated drive around the block.

"God rest *you* merry gentleman," I muttered and turned back to the store.

"Well, that was a nice sale," Lillian murmured looking at her watch. She had to hurry if she would make it to St. Matthew's Christmas Eve service.

"Yes," I growled uncharitably. "If it doesn't come back Wednesday morning."

* * *

I can only speculate what occurred on Christmas morning in the Ridenour home. The magnificent package was unveiled. Mrs. Ridenour was speechless.

And then, "Whatever possessed you, Wesley?"

Mr. Ridenour, nursing the aftermath of his holiday indiscretion, "Well, dear, those gals at the stationery store . . ."

* * *

I have no use for such a garish thing.

Quite predictably, as I unlocked the door the day after Christmas, a Lincoln Town Car pulled up to the curb. I watched from inside the door as Mrs. Ridenour stepped out of the car from the driver's side. She pulled a serviceable brown sweater over her ample bosom. I could swear that a little black thunder cloud hovered over her shoulder. Her steel grey hair, pulled into a severe bun at the nape of her neck accentuated her puckered brow and her pursed lips.

"Come on! Come on!" she seemed to say and gestured irritably to the passenger in the car.

A reluctant Mr. Ridenour emerged and followed her meekly toward the store.

"Come get your lamp," she demanded as soon as she stepped in the door. "Wesley knows that I have no use for such a garish thing. Shame on you for talking him into buying it!"

Chapter 29

THE PANDA EXPRESS

"What in the hell is this!" Max Denton stormed through the front door at closing time. The ding-dong announcing the entry of a customer was overridden by his querulous voice. Max looked like a man dressed for an event, an event somewhat blurred by his presentation. He wore a Hawaiian shirt of fluorescent hues. Plaid Bermuda shorts pulled above his portly waist were held secure by blue suspenders. His eccentric appearance was further enhanced by shiny wing-tip shoes and black nylon socks that reached mid-calf of his spindly white legs. His face was red, his brow moist, his sparse grey hair askew. He obviously had come to the store under hasty and dire circumstances.

"What in the hell is this?" Max repeated. Gripped in his fist was a plastic bag tightly tied to assure that its contents did not slip out. "This came from here, didn't it?"

Sure enough. It was ours. The parcel was tattered and soiled, but our distinctive logo could not be denied. *Chandler Stationers* was emblazoned in red ink across one side of the bag. It contained a lumpy object of some weight.

And did it smell like . . . liver?

* * *

Jimmy Briggs loved Tammy Newton. Their romance began when the two were in high school.

"I'm asking Tammy to the prom," Jimmy confided to

me one Saturday afternoon four years earlier. "I want to buy a bunch of balloons."

"Won't this be fun!" I joshed as I blew up a bouquet of helium balloons for Jimmy. High school kids thought of all kinds of creative ways to avoid face-to-face verbal invitations to significant affairs.

Late that evening Jimmy tied the balloons to a post at Tammy's front door. This was certainly a step above toilet-paper-strewn hedges that were signature prom invitations of many young bucks. Thus, when Tammy stepped onto her front porch the next morning her heart was captured by an array of colorful bobbing missives – red, blue, orange, green, yellow, purple. "Soar with me to the prom!" The invitation was written in permanent marker on each and every balloon.

In honor of the big event Jimmy washed and waxed his Dodge pickup. He swept hay out of the truck bed and vacuumed the cab so that his date would have a proper chariot to the prom. He rented a white dinner jacket, traded his Wranglers for uncuffed black trousers, cleaned his fingernails, and slicked down his straw-thatch hair.

Tammy bought a dark green tea-length party dress off the close-out rack at Janelle's Fashions and she made an appointment at Cassandra's where she indulged in a wash and set followed by a manicure. When she emerged from the salon her long straight hair was twisted into an elegant chignon at the nape of her neck.

The prom was a magical moment in their young lives, and a summer of sweet romance followed.

Come September, Jimmy went south to the University of Arizona where he enrolled in the College of Agriculture.

"I can come home on weekends," Jimmy told me. He was still floating on the euphoria of a star-studded summer.

"It's less than a hundred miles to Tucson," he continued. He purchased a thesaurus for his requisite frosh English class.

Tammy stayed in Chandler where she commuted to Arizona State University and began studies to become an elementary school teacher.

"I'll help Jimmy with his English compositions when he comes home," Tammy said. She paid for a ribbon and correction cassette for her Smith Corona typewriter. As long as Jimmy came home on weekends perhaps love would survive this long-distance romance.

Alas, visits home were not as frequent as either Jimmy or Tammy had imagined. The separation of time and distance took its toll on the relationship, and the semesters rolled around with Jimmy making but cameo appearances in town.

We saw Tammy a bit more often. She began sashaying into the store with Skip Brown. Actually, Tammy sashayed in; Skip lumbered in like a muscle-bound gorilla.

"Skip here is on the Sun Devil football team," Tammy gushed.

She didn't clarify that Skip was a second or even a third string player. There wasn't a chance in the world that Coach Kush would send Skip into an ASU football game this year.

And from the U of A Tucson front, rumor had it that Jimmy was dating a girl from Kappa Kappa Gamma Sorority.

The summer after his sophomore year at the U of A Jimmy earned his pilot's license. A small yellow Cessna parked on a landing strip behind the Briggs Family barns had the same workhorse status on the farm as combines, tractors, and pickup trucks. Jimmy went on to become properly certified as an agricultural pilot and he began to dust crops for the family farms. He flew that Cessna over the land at low altitude and spread fertilizers and pesticides over the vegetation.

Crop dusting was a lucrative endeavor for the young man, and during his junior and senior years at U of A he began to come home more frequently on weekends to perform the task for neighboring farmers.

During his weekends home a spark was reignited between Jimmy and Tammy. However Tammy was confused. Her heart fluctuated between home-again gone-again Jimmy and the macho Skip Brown who, by now, had been elevated to the bench at hotly contested Sun Devil football games.

"What does she see in that dumb jock?" Jimmy lamented one Saturday afternoon.

He had been spraying crops for Tomkins Farms throughout the morning and had come into the store still wearing his crop-dusting attire. He wiped his brow with a red bandana, but he did not wipe the scowl off his freckled face.

"Tammy is *not* available this evening. She has *other* plans!" he mimicked. Jimmy knew that her other plans included the notorious Skip.

Jimmy wanted to impress Tammy. He sought a sure-fire way to turn her heart. He thought about buying another bouquet of balloons reminiscent of the high school prom invitation.

"Nah. It has to be more original than that."

He paused at a glass case displaying an assortment of Precious Moments figurines. These were anemic little figures with big tear-drop eyes that conveyed messages of inspiration, friendship, and love. Two porcelain angels sitting on a cloud caught his attention for a moment. The caption, "Love Goes on Forever" seemed to reflect his sentiment.

"Nah." He passed on it.

What captured his attention was a row of panda bears sitting on a bottom shelf under tubs of gift wrapping bows. We generally did not carry toys in our store. But for some reason we had acquired six dopey-looking pandas. Their wiggly plastic eyes viewed us from every cockamamie direction. They were not soft and cuddly like stuffed animals you give to babies. These were made of stiff wiry textile. If you can imagine Brillo Pads in black and white you get the texture of these pandas. They were hard-stuffed and hefted like bowling balls. Needless to say, these pandas were not hot sellers at the store, and they were beginning to look a bit dusty and shelf-worn.

Jimmy selected one of the pandas. The googly eyes rolled toward its nose. "This will do," he said. He charged the panda to the family's farm account and strode out of the store.

* * *

Max and Ethyl Denton were setting up their back yard for a luau. Ethyl bustled around in her loose turquoise muumuu. Max had just stepped out of the shower and had donned the outrageous shirt Ethyl insisted he wear for the party. He obligingly began carting trays and rearranging chairs to satisfy his wife's entertaining whims. The mood was being set by ukulele music wafting from an RCA Victor phonograph. Guests would be arriving soon. Dips and appetizers were going on the tables. When it got darker, tiki torches would be lit around the pool.

* * *

A yellow Cessna buzzed over the rooftops in Chandler. It circled twice over Hartford Street where Tammy lived. The pilot got his bearings, and then zeroed in on his target. He opened the cockpit window and at a precisely calculated moment pushed a parcel through the opening.

His panda-aim was not as precise as his insecticide-aim. In fact it was a block off. The parcel dropped from the Cessna like a bomb and splatted into Ethyl Denton's chicken liver pâté.

Chapter 30

PHANTOM OF THE STATIONERS

I have never been a cat person. My association with cats has always been at other people's homes where the cat of the manor stalked the premise and pre-empted the best seats and ledges. Certainly, cats came in all manner of gorgeous coats – long hair, short hair, sleek black, fluffy white, spotted, striped, calico, yellow, grey, brown. Their lineage boasted exotic places – Aegean, Angora, Burmese, Egyptian, Manx, Persian, Siamese, Siberian. I was intrigued but not enamored with cats.

A cat is playful. I watched a tabby knock a ball of yarn from my friend's knitting basket. Tabby chased that ball around the kitchen with wild abandon, but I knew that Gloria would eventually have to rewind the string that had made a knotted loopy trail under the table, around the chair legs, behind the sideboard, into the pantry, and out the back door.

A cat is lithe. Every morning as I ate my breakfast toast I observed Queenie, the neighbor's Persian, negotiate my back fence, romp around my yard via the rails, then leap nimbly onto the utility shed roof.

A cat is stubborn. Chester had a perfectly good home across the street, but he spent his days on my front porch. He begrudgingly got up when I opened the door, but not without meowing insolently. Chester immediately resumed residence on the floor mat after the door was closed.

"What's there not to like about cats?" asked Katie, my youngest daughter. She was taking a hiatus from college and had come to work for me in the store.

"Cats are haughty, disdainful, and aloof," I answered.

"Why, cats are just like you," she countered.

Maybe she was right. After all I am a Leo. Maybe I had the disposition of a cat – haughty, disdainful, aloof. At any rate, I took cats in small doses and admired them from afar. Cats seemed to (dis)regard me as I did them.

There was a motley collection of cats that roamed the alley behind Chandler Stationers. They defied the neat little categories established by the Cat Fanciers Association. These felines were skinny, mangy, and ill-natured. Often in the early evening as we closed the store we heard great caterwauling at the back door. A couple of feral Toms were having at it, and they left as evidence matted tufts of fur on the delivery doorstep.

One morning after opening the store I almost stepped in a puddle in the center aisle leading to the office. *Where did that come from?* I instinctively looked up at the ceiling. No leak from above. I hastened to get a mop and bucket to clear the aisle of the puddle. Later in the morning I discovered a calling card of vile nature nestled among the souvenir curios.

"Egad! There is a varmint in the store! I suspect a cat."

I combed the premise. With a yardstick serving as a tapper I went along the shelves hoping to discharge any critter lurking behind book racks, storage boxes, postal scales, expanding files.

Where would a creature seek asylum? The sales floor, furnished with counters, shelves, racks, and spinners offered countless hidey-holes. The storage room on the gift side of the store was loaded with a back-stock of china, crystal, trinkets, albums, and party goods. The other storage room lined with industrial steel shelving housed cases of paper, envelopes, file folders, marker boards, ring binders. The attic was a world unto itself – a dusty jumble of seasonal product, retired display racks, empty boxes, beams and rafters, plus the clap-trap of our lives.

Shelf tapping dislodged no unauthorized tenant.

"Well, maybe it's no longer here," I said hopefully.

But, the next day I found a puddle on a front display counter and an additional calling card on the floor next to the binder racks.

Days passed. Puddles and calling cards dissipated (or I didn't find them) and I was lulled into believing that our night-time prowler had moved onto more lucrative territory. Surely, if our spirit was a warm-blooded fur and bones creature, it was hungry. What had it been surviving on? The pickings were slim in our rest area. A box of crackers, a jar of peanut butter, a can of coffee, all remained untouched. Any other food in the store – lunches and sodas brought by employees – was closed tightly in the refrigerator. I don't believe a cat could have found a self-respecting mouse to eat in Chandler Stationers.

And then, like Zorro, the phantom struck again leaving a brazen and odoriferous mark just inside the front door, an act of open hostility, a declaration of war. In response I mustered the troops, ascended to the armory, mobilized the equipment.

I sought my *modus operandi* among the detritus of the attic. There an arsenal of dubious objects of unknown intent resided in jumbled heaps. I recalled a rusty cage that Jeff had stowed among a tangle of display racks. The object that I wanted was firmly ensconced in the prongs of a wire spinner that had once displayed birthday invitations.

Working my way through the jangle of hooks and prongs I unearthed a snare for some small creature. Perhaps not technically a cat-trap, but it would have to do. An end door-flap lifted. If a critter entered the enclosure it triggered the sensitive catch on the flap. The door slammed shut, and voila, I caught a beastie. If this contraption did its thing expediently, I would have a cat in the morning.

I hauled the awkward cage downstairs with grim determination to catch the interloper. After closing the store Katie and I placed the trap in the wide middle aisle. Before setting the hair-trigger catch, I baited the trap with a can of tuna.

I arrived at the store early the following morning anxious to meet the culprit who had been evading me all week. Something had been in the trap all right. The tuna can was empty. The cage was askew in the aisle, and the door had slammed shut. Some kind of catamount behavior had occurred, but the trap had not contained the critter. I was perplexed. I was bewildered. I was frantic.

Matters culminated that morning when Lillian went into the office storage room. From the corner of her eye she caught a wisp of a tail as it disappeared behind a stack of cartons containing file boxes. She stooped and peered into the dark crevasse between the stack and the wall.

"Here, Kitty Kitty. Here, Kitty Kitty." Lillian crooned. "Here, Kitty Kitty. Here, Kitty Kitty."

A moment later two green eyes glinted in the black void. A nose and whiskers emerged.

"Here, Kitty Kitty. Here, Kitty Kitty."

A gaunt grey feline sidled out of its hidey hole and into Lillian's waiting arms. We returned the phantom of the stationers to the alley where it skittered away.

* * *

"Mew, Mew. Grrr." Faint and faraway.

"Do you have a cat in your back room?" Mrs. Dawson asked me.

"No, we don't have cats in the store." I replied, my fingers crossed, as I recalled the unwelcome phantom we had dislodged a few weeks earlier.

"Well I hear a cat." Mrs. Dawson was adamant.

"Mew, Mew. Grrr."

I could no longer ignore the niggling sensation that I, too, occasionally heard rustling and mewling that seemed to come from the wall that separated the stock room from the sales floor. Originally the sounds were almost imperceptible, but they were definitely getting louder.

I hauled out the tall ladder and began an unscientific assessment of the situation. I put my ear to the wall at various intervals. I called Katie to assist me. She repeated my strategy. We were both convinced that the sounds centralized over the door to the stock room. But what to do?

"We have to tear into the wall," I said.

"What if we hit something?" Katie shuddered.

"We'll have to be careful," I answered.

With rudimentary tools – hammer and screwdriver– I timidly created a ding in the plaster over the door. Dust rained on Katie who stood below me. Using the screwdriver as a chisel and then a wedge, little by little I increased the size of the hole in the wall creating an opening big enough for a hand to go through.

"I think they are to the right of this hole," I said to Katie. "But, I can't see them. Kittens?"

"How many?," Katie asked.

"I have no idea." I cringed at the thought of reaching into the void. If cats could give birth within the walls no telling what other denizens skittered among the studs and joists "Will you get them out?" I asked her.

When you worked for family you signed on for whatever came down the pike. And this was Katie's current job assignment.

"I won't reach into that hole with my bare hands." Katie shuttered.

"Run over to the drug store and buy a pair of work gloves," I replied. "Leather if they have them."

Errand complete and canvas gauntlets (leather was not available) shielding her hands, Katie climbed the ladder. She stuck her arm warily through the opening. Nothing glommed onto her appendage. She didn't have far to reach. She accomplished the task by feel. Ultimately Katie pulled five scrawny kittens of variegated color from their lair within the wall. Their eyes were still closed. They hissed softly.

Lillian, who was in and out of the back room as Katie and I conducted this operation, was first to see a writhing mass of fur in a cardboard box.

"Oh, look at this adorable calico," Lillian cooed. "A little girl, I believe." She cradled the kitten in the palm of her hand as she examined its private parts to determine its sex. I tried a similar procedure with the other infants. Boy or girl? I could not tell the difference.

Now I had another problem. What to do with the kittens?

"We must feed them," Lillian said. "Probably with baby bottles."

"Well . . ." I hedged. I really didn't want to get into the cat raising business.

"Aw, Mom, they're just babies," Katie wheedled. "Let me get some baby bottles and milk at the drug store."

I sighed and handed over ten dollars from petty cash to apply to the cat mission. Even insensitive Susan had a twinge of compassion for the babes taken from their refuge and mama cat who would return to find her litter gone.

As Katie made her second dash to the drug store, Lillian busied herself lining the box with rags from our housekeeping supply.

Thus armed with five small baby bottles and a quart of milk, Katie and Lillian spent the afternoon trying to teach their new charges how to suckle. The kittens licked the rubber nipples cautiously but seemed to want nothing to do with the improvised nursing system.

By now customers coming into the store knew that we had retrieved kittens from within the walls. Something about a helpless kitten stirs the hardest of hearts. We began to receive offers to adopt the cunning things. When one lady declared that she would like to take the calico, Lillian spoke up.

"I've already claimed Calico."

Lillian! What in heaven's name will you do with a cat!

She must have read my thoughts. "Larry will take care of Calico for me while she's little and I'm at work,"

Lillian said. She was referring to her neighbor and fellow church member who was a cat fancier himself. I thought it was pretty brassy to assume that Larry would take on an infant kitten of indeterminate lineage whose eyes were not yet open. Who knew what kind of infirmities it brought into the world?

By the end of the day four kittens had been packed off to unsuspecting homes. And Calico left in a rag-lined box to Lillian's condo.

You can't take the alley out of the cat.

Well, Larry, compassionate soul that he was, took on the task of taming the feral feline and did a commendable job of getting it through the infant stages. After Calico filled out she was a rather pretty cat. But I know she was a disappointment to Lillian.

Lillian wanted a lap cat, a pet to come home to after a long day's work. Calico was a loner. During the day when Lillian was at work, Calico paced the apartment and scratched the furniture. She prowled along counter tops, shelves, and window sills, upsetting plants, books, and figurines. When Lillian was at home, Calico sulked under the bed. She skittered around the hand that fed her, arched her back, spit, and communicated through hisses and growls.

Nature or nurture? I don't know what went wrong with Calico. The intention behind adopting her was noble, but Calico never became fully civilized. She seemed to prove the adage:

You can take the cat out of the alley, but you can't take the alley out of the cat.

Chapter 31

TO EVERY THING THERE IS A SEASON
and a time to every purpose under heaven
Ecclesiastes 3:1

Timing is everything. In life and in business. On the continuum of time there are two extremes, a positive and a negative, an up and a down, an *either* and an *or*. Win . . .lose. Give . . . take. Laugh . . . cry. The one thing we can count on as time passes is change.

We had six clocks in our home and no two had precisely the same time. However, our home life was regulated by an old grandfather clock that stood sentinel beside the dining room door. Tick. Tock. Tick. Tock. Its pendulum swung to and fro as seconds marched into eternity. Every fifteen minutes throughout the day its Westminster Chime notified us of the passage of time: time to put the coffee on, time to wake the children, time to send them off to school, or time to hand Jeff his lunch pail as he marched out the door for another day at the store.

On occasions when we forgot to wind the clock on a Sunday morning our timing for Monday was thrown askew. The doleful chime marked minutes further and further behind schedule until time stood still. The coffee got cold before we drank it; the children overslept; and Jeff found himself bolting out the door with or without his lunch pail.

Our business life was regulated by a fourteen-inch wall clock that hung over the doorway to the back office. Unless storm or some kind of mishap along the power grid knocked out the electricity, the rhythm of the store depended on that clock.

157

A time to open . . . and a time to close

"Open." Every morning at 8:00 a.m. Viktor flipped the laminated sign that signaled the store was ready for trade. He bustled about setting up the cash register for business, and began assembling orders for his daily delivery route.

"Closed." Every evening at 6:00 p.m. Jeff flipped the sign to its reverse side. He removed the cash drawer from the register, counted the take for the day, and prepared the drawer for the next day's business.

Six-days-a-week, year-in and year-out. Variations in procedure occurred on Viktor's day off (Saturday) or when Jeff was away (likely gone hunting). But, protocol was the same. Open at 8:00 a.m. Close at 6:00 p.m. Occasionally, I stepped in for Jeff. Or perhaps Dorcas attended to either the opening or closing routine. We were fortunate to have dependable, versatile employees adept at multitasking.

A time to buy . . . and a time to sell

A semi-truck pulled up to the back door. Viktor scratched his head as he watched the driver hop out and begin carting untold boxes into the receiving area. "Oh my goodneth," he lamented. "Wheah will we put all thith thtuff?" His mantra never ceased.

Dad's philosophy, in order to get the best bang for our bucks and thus the best prices for our customers, was to order in quantity. For most of our office supplies he dealt directly with manufacturers who dispensed their products by the gross. From clasp envelopes to ring binders, from paper clips to file folders, from report covers to desk files, our stock rooms had as much merchandise as our sales floor. This was a decade of spiraling inflation; with every order placed prices increased. There was a distinct advantage in buying earlier rather than later.

The philosophy of retail businesses has changed in the ensuing years. Today, with instant communication and fast delivery options, stores keep very little back stock. Their total inventory is on display on the sales floor – a sensible trend, for merchandise rotates and remains fresh.

But during our days in business there was a significant delay between ordering merchandise from a manufacturer, and having it delivered to the back door. "Anticipate what the customer needs and have it on hand," Dad proclaimed as he ordered another pallet of mimeograph paper that we would be tripping over for the next six months.

A time to keep . . . and a time to give away

On occasion Dad's philosophy of ordering prodigious quantities backfired. One year following Christmas, a Grand Bull from the Moose Lodge came in seeking party hats, masks, and noise makers for their New Year's Eve Party. Our wimpy selection of New Year's party goods from Hallmark was not nearly enough to supply the big Moose gala on such short notice.

"I had no idea that New Year's was such a big wing-ding around here," Dad muttered. "We won't be caught short next year." And come the following September he ordered cases of glittery headgear – top hats, cone hats, tiaras. And boxes of noise makers – whistles, horns, and rattles. And sparkly masks and feather boas.

But never again did we have an opportunity to outfit the Moose Lodge or any other lodge, for that matter, with New Year's Eve festive gear. Those cases moved up and down from the attic season after season until we had to acknowledge a marketing disaster.

"It's time to pass this hoop-la along," Jeff groused. And we carted it away. Any lodge or brotherhood seeking New Year's party supplies got a gonga deal at the local Salvation Army thrift store.

A time to work . . . and a time to play

Dorcas officially retired. "I'm sure you'll agree that twenty-eight years is a long time to devote to one store," she said when she picked up her last pay check. "Grover and I plan to travel a bit."

Dorcas had paid her dues. She actually had been semi-retired for the past five years, working part time and calling the shots for when she would come in to work. This had been an equitable arrangement for us, for Dorcas had continued to keep her pet sections in the store fully stocked and in military order.

We would have to appoint someone else to assume control of the shelves of albums, the paper party goods, the gift wrap and bows, and the greeting card racks.

A time to hire . . .

Through the years other employees stepped up to the plate. Many were matrons who worked because they needed the money. We found them invaluable, for they were dependable, hard working, and trainable. Most did not know twit about office products before stepping into the job (nor did I, for that matter), but they gamely rolled up their sleeves and accepted any mundane task that came down the pike.

Two special ladies rode the waves of the store until the end, Lillian and Alexa. I introduced Lillian in earlier chapters. Lillian, in her penury circumstances, claimed to be locked into a life of mandatory labor. However, I suspected, with her gregarious nature and busy-body tendency, the store was her social scene. Where else could she keep a pulse on the community?

Alexa was married to a prominent land developer. She worked for the fun of it. And getting a bit of personal income sweetened the pot. In her salon coiffed hair, her Calvin Klein coordinates, and her Capezio mini heels Alexa brought a touch of culture and class to the store. She had a knack for creating eclectic table-top displays using disparate merchandise from around the store. Alexa was the natural candidate to step into the role of guru of the greeting cards, albums, and party goods that Dorcas had vacated. In subsequent years Lillian and Alexa became the store's mainstays as well as my lifelong friends.

Jeff had groomed a series of stock boys along the way. The bar was set by Tomás, the first young man we hired from the high school work-study program. Quick, diligent, conscientious, Tomás was the kind of boy we needed to sift through incoming deliveries to get product ready for the shelves. He kept the floor mopped, the windows washed, the sidewalk swept. He climbed high ladders, wrestled heavy parcels, and was unfailingly polite to the ladies. This was a lot to expect from a boy who came to work after school. Tomás, the son of Mexican migrant workers, was the first in his family to finish high school. We were proud of him when he went on to community college. And we reaped additional benefits when Tomás stayed on as our stock boy through his junior college years.

Other fine young men followed. Philip gave us three years of exemplary service before he joined the Navy. When his military stint was over he came back to work at the store for a while until he got his land-legs under him and settled into the university.

And a time to fire . . .

We did have occasional doozies among the ranks. But they didn't last long, their names quickly forgotten. One stock-boy-in-training disappeared out the back door of the store as police came in the front door. We later learned that this young man was part of a teen-age ring found vandalizing construction sites. He never returned to work. We removed him from the payroll.

One woman that I was responsible for hiring had a warrant out for her arrest. She had skipped out of Reno with forgery charges against her. During her brief employ at Chandler Stationers, the cash register money count consistently less than the register tape tally, usually by about twenty dollars. Although I had niggling suspicions of her, I did not have any concrete evidence that she was responsible for the chronic shortage. The issue self-corrected after the police arrived at her apartment with the Nevada citation and she returned to Reno.

A time to be born . . . and a time to die

Viktor's health began to worsen. "Wheeze, wheeze, gasp, gasp." The time came when the little inhaler did not relieve his breathing problems. Other serious health issues ensued. He began missing days, and then weeks of work. He shriveled before our eyes.

"The doctor telth me I muth quit work," Viktor told Jeff and then Dad when he submitted his resignation. "I thpent my whole caweeah on thith vewwy block." I believe he sounded a bit wistful.

Viktor had more that forty cumulative years' employment associated with the stationery store under his belt, with us and with the Williams before us. He was entitled to step into Social Security and Medicare and enjoy some well-earned leisure hours.

We were stunned when just a few months after his retirement Viktor died.

"We didn't fully understand the magnitude of his health problems," I said to Jeff.

He was an odd duck," Jeff replied, "but he was dependable."

A delegation from Chandler Stationers sat stiffly along a pew near the back of the sanctuary at St. Mary's Church. Unfamiliar with Catholic ceremony, we found ourselves observers of the highly ritualistic service in a church that had been an important part of Viktor's life.

Viktor's wife, Estelle, sat grimly alone on the front pew, a pathetic testament to Viktor's lack of family ties. Sadly, we realized that the stationery store and its customers had been his closest link to a family.

As I looked about the congregation at St. Mary's Church I was touched to see customers of the store scattered among the modestly occupied pews. Viktor's delivery and order-taking routes had put him in touch with a wide span of the community – from grocery store magnates to carry-out boys, from farmers to field hands, as well as doctors, lawyers, insurance agents, car dealers, and secretaries. More than a few had always assumed that Viktor was the owner of the stationery store. And Viktor had done little to dissuade that impression.

Viktor had come to Chandler as a young man where he hoped to find a respite for his multiple allergies. He had made his mark.

A time to tear down. . .

As Chandler Stationers experienced an undulating staff, the downtown square went through ups and downs in the name of progress. Progress is a double-edged sword. Progress involves disruption. Disruption creates a loss of business.

Streets widened. A drainage system put in. Lights installed. Parking lots created. The park re-landscaped. The façade around the square remodeled. And remodeled again. Buildings razed and a city complex built. Every step of progress involved great lumbering machines, deep trenches, mountains of dirt, and deafening noise. Customers had a difficult time finding parking spots and negotiating construction debris.

And a time to build up. . .

Chandler was moving into a new era. In 1967 we had stepped into a bucolic community of 9,500 people who relied on businesses around the town square for their personal and business needs. Now, strip malls were sprouting up along main thoroughfares into Chandler – grocery stores, hardware stores, sporting goods stores, fabric shops, plus exotic businesses like aquarium supply stores and modeling agencies – and the population of Chandler had multiplied ten times.

The only constant on the continuum of time is change. Change was happening.

Chapter 32

DUCHÂTEAU, INC.

Clerks scattered when he came in the door. Along with the cheerful ding-dong that alerted us that the front door had opened, in wafted an odious stench, a medley of wood smoke, diesel oil, cat urine, sewer gas, and plain old body odor. We knew that Duchâteau brought his weekly trade to the store.

I never knew if Duchâteau was his real name. It was the moniker under which he operated. He materialized at the cash register on a hot July afternoon. The blistering 110° outside temperature was magnified by sizzling reflections from the sidewalk. A cloud of dust, heat, and flies accompanied this apparition into the store.

He might have been the Lost Dutchman who wandered throughout the Superstition Mountains seeking the purported Peralta Gold. A wiry untamed beard framed his face. Brown drizzles at the corners of his mouth suggested that his tobacco of recreation was Cannonball Plug.

His greasy felt hat had a wide brim that hung downward somewhat obscuring his ears, but tendrils of matted hair poked from under it at odd angles. Most alarming was a hole that penetrated its crown front to back. One could imagine an arrow removing this chapeau or perhaps the bullet from a .30-06. Between the hat and the beard there was little to see of the mystery customer's face. Bushy brows, bloodshot eyes, bad teeth.

"I need to place an order," he growled.

"Yes sir," I replied and turned aside hoping to gasp a bit of untainted air.

"I want you to make me some rubber stamps." He dug into his vest pocket and pulled out a tightly folded scrap of paper.

I reached for an order form we used to procure rubber stamps.

His hands twitched violently as he attempted to smooth the crumpled paper over the counter. It had been a long time since his fingers had seen a basin of water. His long chipped nails were rimmed in black. The thumb of his right hand had been amputated at the knuckle

Several pencil lines were scratched over the paper in irregular childish script. The top line said **DUCHÂTEAU INC.** He wanted to have a rubber stamp made in big letters. I showed him the lettering styles available, and he selected a bold Helvetica type. The size font that he chose meant that the stamp would stretch across five inches. That meant he would need a big stamp pad to accommodate the stamp. But he assured me that he did not need the pad.

He went on to the next item on his list. **Acct # 87482.** And I dutifully prepared a second order for a rubber stamp, this time in a smaller font.

And the next item. **Research project C79 SECRET**
And the next item. **Formula cX63ad**

All-in-all my new customer ordered seven unfathomable rubber stamps.

"It usually takes five days for special-order stamps to come in," I told him.

"That's fine." He nodded curtly. "I'll be back next week."

"Uh . . . It's customary to make a deposit on special orders," I stammered. I doubted that I would see the old man again, and I didn't want to be stuck for seven odd-ball rubber stamps.

He extracted a handful of bills from the depths of his

dungaree pockets. "What'll it be?" he asked.

"Uh . . . Twelve dollars will be half," I replied. And my new customer sifted through a wad of limp Jacksons, Hamiltons, Lincolns, and Washingtons to pay cash on the barrelhead for half the amount due on the stamps. I issued him a receipt for the transaction and prepared the unusual order for fax transmittal to our supplier of rubber stamps.

Hereafter we referred to this mystery customer as Duchâteau, a fancy French name when translated meant *one who lives in a castle*. Certainly, the name evoked an element of *savoir faire*. But we figured he most likely lived in a desert camp far from any facilities to perform ordinary ablutions.

A inscrutable routine began. Every Friday afternoon Duchâteau bounced into town, the sole passenger in a dented green pickup driven by a Pima Indian from the reservation. He picked up the previous week's order, settling his account in full with the wad of damp bills in his pocket.

Then he began again with a crumpled paper from his vest pocket and an equally bizarre series of terms to be made into rubber stamps. Each week the transaction was sealed with half-payment in cash meticulously counted and pressed into my palms.

NO ADMITTANCE
Formula fY72ad
Expires 7/19/2036 *(Hmmm. Fifty years in the future)*

Duchâteau's uniform did not vary from week to week. If anything, his body and his garb became more and more grimy. Denim dungarees, stiff with grease and grunge, were held up by green suspenders. A shirt of indeterminate color was long-sleeved and ragged. And a dirt-smeared, multi-pocketed vest served as a filing system for his business endeavors.

Occasionally the task of preparing Duchâteau's orders fell to Alexa whom we had the good fortune of hiring after

Dorcas retired. Because Alexa brought a touch of culture and class to our store, she was a natural to help customers with social endeavors. Often I gave her the task of assisting brides who were ordering wedding invitations or with doyennes of the community who were planning festivities and needed decorations for the events.

Helping Duchâteau was a bit beyond her call of duty, but Alexa gamely tackled his orders and turned his indecipherable gibberish into orders for rubber stamps.

High Priority
FKPJM-HFDCX
CO2 727

The old geezer obviously enjoyed having the demure lady assist him.

One day Duchâteau placed his garbled order, and then he whispered to Alexa in a gravelly voice, "She died. I woke up . . . and she was dead."

"Oh!" Startled, Alexa neglected to find out who "she" was. Was "she" a wife? An Indian woman? A dog? At any rate, from that time on Alexa disappeared into the back room when Duchâteau walked in the front door, and it became my sole duty to prepare the inexplicable rubber stamp orders. I couldn't afford to lose an employee over this reprobate, yet, he was a paying customer, and we were making a bit of profit off the old coot.

[QRT 26 HBT] : 3[TRQ JK]
Confidential
X Approved

Duchâteau once leaned over the counter and whispered conspiratorially in my ear, "The news . . . is about . . . to break."

"The . . . news . . . is . . . about . . . to break?" I repeated; my eyes rolled heavenward.

"Yes . . . the news is about to break." Duchâteau lowered his voice. "I'm about to release this-here formula to the medical community." He paused dramatically. "I have found a cure . . ." His voice dropped another decibel. ". . . for all the pestilence in the world."

I'm about to release this-here formula

"A cure . . . for all the pestilence in the world?" I blithered.

"The formulas I give you today will unlock the mysteries of all disease."

And he gave me a list of his most secret prescriptions to make into rubber stamps. Some of them sounded a bit familiar. But, I was rusty on algebraic and chemical equations.

E=MC2
sin (*wq*) *T* 2*p*
Ag$_2$O
V=bh3

After this peculiar revelation, numerous weeks, even months, passed. Duchâteau's last order rotated to the back of the drawer where we kept special-order stamps. Ah well. He had paid his deposit, so we hadn't lost any money on the deal.

Another hot summer afternoon and the door bell alerted us that someone had walked in the store. I was restocking the pen case and nodded to a stranger who approached me.

"I've come to get my rubber stamps."

By jingo! It was Duchâteau! Shaved and shorn, an anemic band across the bottom of his face looked like the skin of a freshly plucked chicken. A couple of small adhesive strips covered recent razor nicks in his chin. He was wearing khaki pants and a plaid shirt that must have just come off the shelves at Penney's. They still bore the creases of newly purchased garments. And he wore a crisp straw fedora.

"I'll bet you thought I forgot," he cackled.

Cleaned up, Duchâteau had rather nice regular features. A strong jaw line, a straight nose, and twinkly eyes. Of course, he was still rough around the edges, and his teeth were still bad. After all, you can't make a silk cravat out of tow sack.

I handed him his purchase. "It's been a while," I said.

Duchâteau reached into his pocket and pulled out the inimitable wad of bills. Twenties, tens, fives, and ones – a moist clump in his hand. He counted out exact cash for what was due on the rubber stamps.

I prudently refrained from asking if the formulas on these stamps were still going to the medical community.

"Thank you for holding these until I could get back to pick them up," he said.

He did not place a new order.

Chapter 33

ASIAN INVASION

Alexa and I were unpacking a carton of souvenirs that had been delivered to the back door of the stockroom. Arizona souvenirs – plates decorated with cactus and roadrunners, mugs declaring *But It's a Dry Heat*, shot glasses bearing the image of the Arizona flag, key chains with bangles shaped like boots and Stetsons. This twaddle was popular with winter visitors as well as the tourist crowd that settled in at the San Marcos Hotel.

"This is sure a mess," I complained. Flimsy cardboard cartons housing the merchandise were cushioned with excelsior that scattered over the floor and was being tracked throughout the store.

Most of the items were packaged in dozens. A dozen rubber scorpions, a dozen pewter spoons with rattlesnakes coiling around the handles, a dozen desert snow globes (*Snow globes! In the desert!*). Straw-like particles of excelsior clung statically to the merchandise.

All of this souvenir stuff was made overseas and shipped across the Pacific to wholesalers who passed it on to us.

"Ah, here are some salt and pepper shakers," I exclaimed. I proceeded to unearth one more box – novelty salt and pepper shakers created in the shape of Arizona according to the label on the box.

These decorative condiment pieces bore simplified strata of three regions of Arizona's ecological terrain, the desert, the mountains, and the high plateaus. ARIZONA was carefully painted across the face of each piece.

But whoa! Something was wrong. This was not Arizona. These salt and pepper shakers were molded in the shape of Utah, our neighbor to the north.

Arizona? Utah? Ah-so! Someplace in American west. What difference did it make?

Made in Japan

* * *

"That doesn't look like anything we would normally carry," I said to the West Coast Distributer who had been going through his catalog with me.

"I guarantee that these little balls will sell. I will take them back if I am wrong."

The item in question seemed like an odd thing for Mr. Samuel to be hawking, for generally his product line was desk-top items.

He was trying to get me to buy a display of glow-in-the-dark rubber balls that bounced to super heights. They were packaged by the gross. Their display was a large collapsible wire basket on wheels.

"Put them beside the cash register and every kid in town will get one."

That was the trouble. Every salesman assured us that if we put his product beside the cash register it would blow out of the store.

What the heck? The glow-in-the-dark balls were inexpensive. We didn't carry many amusements for children. And a lot of children did come in with their parents.

"I *will* return the balls," I assured Mr. Samuel, "if they are a bomb."

Much to my surprise the glow-in-the-dark balls were wildly popular.

"We have a winner here," I conceded to Mr. Samuel on one of his later visits. "I will order another display."

However, our entire profit in glow-in-the dark balls was wiped out in one fell swoop when a little renegade from the Indian reservation came into the store with his mother. He lobbed onto one of those balls. We watched in slo-mo horror as the ball arced over a display of music boxes and headed toward the front window. On a top shelf, a majestic display of art-glass shimmered in the afternoon sun. The aim could not have been truer had the urchin tried. The ball slammed into a hobnail vase that formed the focal point of the display. Green glass exploded taking with it candy dishes, pitchers, compotes, candlesticks, and glass slippers. Kaleidoscopic chards of glass – cobalt, ruby, violet, topaz – rained on the floor below.

The glow-in-the-dark ball ricocheted against the wall, rolled back toward the counter, circled lamely, and settled at my feet.

Made in Taiwan

* * *

The Surgeon General had declared that smoking was detrimental to our health. More and more *No Smoking* signs were going up in offices and work areas around the community. Some *No Smoking* signs were on thirty-six inch florescent posters. Others were discreet little placards to prop on desks. We carried a variety of these signs.

At one summer gift show Alexa and I were browsing through the display of an importer who carried fine linens – table cloths, napkins, handkerchiefs, pillow shams, and the like.

"We could use these doilies and table runners for display under our glassware," Alexa said.

"It is hard to find ladies' handkerchiefs these days," I added. I was looking at a display of dozens of delicately embroidered hankies fluttering from a tabletop spinner. "I think I will order some of these along with the doilies and table runners."

The importer also carried elaborate needlepoint tapestries – floral designs, landscapes, animal and mythological motifs. A lot of intricate hand work was involved in creating these exquisite items.

Then my eye caught an elegant little sign. It measured about six inches long and two inches high. It hung from a woven cord. Tiny needlepoint stitches created a colorful floral design around the border. In equally fine stitches the message *No Smoking* stood white against the black crewel background. A boudoir item. I could think of several ladies who would hang this sign in their parlor rather than one those industrial florescent ones. Surely we could sell six which was the minimum order.

In time the order was delivered. We unpacked the parcel, anticipating the fresh look that the items would bring to our gift displays. Doilies, table runners, and hankies were crisp and bright, just as they were at the show.

But, the *No Smoking* signs . . . There were individual variations as you might expect in hand crafted pieces. However . . .

Every one of the signs read NO SNOKING.

M? N? Smoking? Snoking? The designer of the pattern could see no difference.

Six *No Snoking* signs stitched by six women huddled around dim light in a Dhaka factory.

Made in Bangladesh

* * *

Nell Andrews served on the City Council. When her term ended and she decided not to run again she was presented with a Montblanc pen by her colleagues. Montblanc was one of the most exclusive writing instruments on the market. Its name and logo were inspired by Mont Blanc, the highest alp in Europe. A presentation of this magnitude was a testament of the high esteem in which Nell's peers held her. We carried a small selection of the classic Montblanc Meisterstuck line – fountain pen, ballpoint pen, rollerball, and pencil. And, of course, we carried the refills to go in them. Sales of Montblanc pens were few and far between. We had not sold a Montblanc writing instrument for a long time.

"I've never had a ballpoint run out of ink so quickly," Nell said. She had been telling me about the presentation at the City Council meeting. "Already, I need a new refill."

"Fine." I took the pen. "We have Montblanc refills. Do you want blue ink or black?"

The pen was a heavy well-balanced instrument that bore a white stylized star on its cap. This design was supposed to emulate the snow on top of the famous mountain for which it was named.

"Blue ink please," she replied.

I unscrewed the cap. Nell had already removed the deplete refill and thrown it away. But that was no problem. Because this was a Montblanc pen, it would take a Montblanc refill. Sometimes people wanted refills for their no-name pens. If the existing refill had been removed it was hard to know which of our dozens of refill brands would fit in the pen. In such a case, trial and error was the only way to outfit a no-name pen with a useable refill.

I took a blue Montblanc ballpoint refill from the case and proceeded to slip it into the pen. Puzzlement. The Montblanc refill would not fit into the pen Nell Andrews brought in.

When a Montblanc refill would not go into a Montblanc pen something was wrong.

This pen was a knock-off. Nell Andrews had been awarded a handsome replication of a Montblanc pen for her service on the city council. A side-by-side comparison of this pen and a true Montblanc revealed subtle differences.

I sold Nell a seventy-nine cent generic refill that fit many odd-ball pens on the market.

Made in China

Chapter 34

ANGEL UNAWARE

Often on a Saturday morning Amanda Dixon came into the store to purchase glue, paints, and construction paper so the children in her Sunday school class could craft projects that would bring her lessons to life. Today she pondered two sizes of Crayola boxes that were on our shelves.

"I want a new box of crayons," Amanda said. "The colors that the children have been using are worn down to the nubbins."

"There is something magical about a brand-new box of sharp waxy crayons," I replied. "When I was a girl I tried to see how long a box would last before I broke a crayon. Usually, not long."

"Yes, kids are pretty heavy-handed with crayons. The children really don't need twenty-four colors," Amanda continued. "If I bought two sixteen-packs they would get a nice variety, and there would be less squabbling over the colors." Amanda obviously had a good way with children.

"How are you feeling?" I alluded to the visible baby-bump that had transformed Amanda's slim body.

"It should be about three weeks." Amanda groaned and arched her back. "My back still aches, but I no longer have indigestion. The doctor says that the baby has dropped. Everything is on track."

"How about Josh?"

Amanda's face fell. "He calls occasionally. But, like everybody else, I keep track of what's going on through the evening news."

Amanda paid for her purchase. As she waddled out the door, I sighed. She had a strong support group. Amanda grew up in the Blessed Redeemer Church. Her father served on the Council of Elders, and her mother presided over of the Women's Bible Society. Amanda taught the second grade Sunday school class. The congregation embraced her. We had watched Amanda grow through this Christian environment, and she was now a kind and gracious young lady.

Amanda was married to Josh. Two years ago she had been in the store to order wedding invitations.

"It won't be an elaborate affair," she said. "We will invite congregation members through the church newsletter. We only need a few invitations to send to friends and relatives outside the church." She ordered twenty-five invitations embossed with hearts and bells.

"Nelda D'mowski will bake our cake in her home kitchen," Amanda told me on a subsequent visit. She purchased a miniature bride and groom made of stiff plastic to top the frosted confection. Then she chose paper plates and napkins from our wedding collection for the reception.

Members of the Blessed Redeemer Church followed, in turn, to purchase wedding cards for the couple. "Congratulations to the newly married couple." "May your marriage be blessed with faith, joy, and love." "May you be as rich in life as you are in love." After the popular event we had to replenish our wedding cards.

At the simple home-spun service, the pews at the Blessed Redeemer Church filled with well-wishers. A reception followed in the fellowship hall where the blushing bride and the awkward groom cut into a three-tiered cake piled with scallops of white frosting roses. Cake was served and the young couple fled the church under a hail of rice. They took a week-long honeymoon to Flagstaff where they stayed at an economical Motel 6 and made side trips to the Grand Canyon, to Sunset Crater, and to sites of interest on the Navajo Reservation.

"We have a duplex apartment on Ivanhoe," Amanda told me upon their return from the honeymoon. "Josh has gone back to his job as a lineman for Arizona Public Service. I'm still working part-time for Dr. Melton."

Now, two years later, Amanda was going to have a baby. The Bible Society planned a shower, and the matrons of the church came to the store as a committee to select accoutrements for the event.

"Not pink or blue," argued Mrs. Stapleton. "Amanda doesn't know if the baby will be a girl or a boy." Instead they selected yellow bunnies and white daisies as their theme.

We had a run on baby gifts prior to the big event. Mrs. Myles, Amanda's mother, purchased *A Keepsake Album*. Amanda would be able to keep a record of key events in her baby's life on beautifully illustrated vellum pages. The minister's wife bought a gift book entitled *Prayers for Baby*. The second grade Sunday school class pooled their resources and sent little Peggy Drew and Alice Betters to the store to make a gift selection. The girls looked at lace baby bibs and silver spoons before deciding that they had just enough money to buy a nakedy kewpie doll figurine. "This will be perfect," Peggy giggled. "You can't tell if it is a boy or a girl."

Everything was falling into place.

The problem was that Josh was not around for the impending birth. He was grubbing about an Arabian desert in camouflage. His National Guard unit had been called and he was deployed to Iraq.

Because a number of local young men and women had been sent into that deadly skirmish the community felt a special connection to what was called Operation Desert Storm. When the conflict broke out we set a tree branch near the front door of Chandler Stationers. And under that branch we placed a bucket of ribbons – yellow ribbons, which throughout history have been symbols of faithfulness and waiting for lovers to return from war. When customers came in the door they took ribbons from the bucket and laced the bough with yellow tendrils emulating a popular song of the day.

Amanda had her baby, a little girl named Joshlynn in honor of her absent father. The congregation of the Blessed Redeemer Church surged into the store to purchase New Baby Cards. "Congratulations on your new arrival." "Best wishes to you and your new little one." "May the joy of parenting bring you a lifetime of laughter and happiness." Then we replenished our selection of new baby cards.

Three weeks after Joshlynn was born Amanda brought her to the store. The clerks gathered round to admire the new baby.

"Ooh"

"How precious."

"She looks just like you."

An angel of a child slumbered in her baby carrier. Translucent eyelids and blond lashes fluttered as she slept. Amanda glowed. Motherhood served her well.

Then, one night, the inexplicable happened. Baby Joshlynn died. Paramedics who raced to the duplex on Ivanhoe were unable to revive the infant who died while sleeping. SIDS (Sudden Infant Death Syndrome) they called it.

Members of the Blessed Redeemer Church surged into the store again, this time seeking cards that expressed their condolences. "Deepest Sympathies." "Strength and Comfort." "Our Prayers Are With You."

* * *

I left the store in time to slip in to the last pew at the Blessed Redeemer Church before the service began. The rows ahead of me were filled. A small lace-lined coffin reposed before the altar.

The minister led the family into the sanctuary from a side door. Elder Myles and Mrs. Myles, Amanda's parents, filed in with grim, stoic faces. Amanda, wearing a simple dress of dove grey, was ashen, her eyes puffy from hours of tears. Beside her, gripping her arm was a young man dressed in desert camouflage. A young man, granted a leave of compassion, had been flown to Arizona to attend the funeral of his namesake.

Chapter 35

SECRETARY FOR LIFE

I had left my car at Sawyer's Service Center for its regular oil change and lube and whatever else mechanics do under the hoods of little Ford Contours. After work, I walked two blocks from the store to retrieve my vehicle. Sam Sawyer, proprietor and head mechanic presented me with my keys and my bill. As ever, I was dumbfounded by the charges that added up for things I didn't know were wrong with my vehicle. Brake pads, radiator hose, clamps, coolant, engine air filter. I gulped and handed Sam my VISA.

"You are now a privileged member of the Auto Care Club," Sam said as he gave me my receipt.

I was leery of joining clubs. During a period of intellectual enlightenment I had joined the Classical Book of the Month Club. I now possessed an entire bookcase full of unread volumes gathering dust – from Homer to Aeschylus, from Dante to Rabelais, from Wordsworth to Tennyson, from Hawthorne to Thoreau. Not until the book club got into Russian fiction of the Renaissance did I call a halt to the onslaught of tomes arriving monthly in my mailbox, thus severing my membership in the Classical Book of the Month Club.

"The Auto Care Club." I balked. "I don't have time for another club." It seemed that every club I joined voted me secretary – perhaps because I have the tidy, precise penmanship of an English teacher and take copious notes. When my children were in school I had been secretary of the

P.T.A. as well as secretary of the high school band boosters. I served as secretary of the women's fellowship at my church and secretary of my P.E.O. chapter. At the moment I was serving as secretary of our neighborhood block watch organization. I'd make a hell of a secretary for an Auto Care Club. I didn't understand twit about what went on in the bowels of an automobile.

"As a member of the Auto Care Club, every time you have your car serviced you will receive a ten-dollar coupon good for your next oil and lube job," Sam continued. He then gave me an imposing certificate that entitled me to ten dollars off my next service at his shop. Ten dollars was a drop in the bucket in the scheme of auto maintenance. However, ten dollars was ten dollars. And I didn't have to take notes.

"Thank you," I said and tucked the receipt and certificate into my purse.

"Oh, by the way," Sam stopped me before I walked out the door. "I've been meaning to ask you . . . The Downtown Merchants' Association needs a new secretary. The board thought you would be a good one. Will you take on the job?"

Well, I didn't end up as secretary of the Auto Care Club, but I did end up as secretary of the Chandler Downtown Merchants' Association.

This meant I had two more things to put on my calendar – a monthly board meeting in the Arizona Public Service staff room and a monthly breakfast meeting at Serrano's Restaurant for the general membership. As secretary I was to keep track of what went on at these meetings. It also turned out that the secretary was to send out monthly bulletins to remind members of upcoming meetings and events. And, when new businesses settled in the area the secretary was to personally invite them to participate in the association. Maybe it would have been easier to be secretary of the Auto Care Club.

I had seen an Open for Business sign on the window

of a shop in a strip mall on the north side of town. This would be my fledgling endeavor to invite a new business to come to our association meetings. I pulled into one of the parking spots in front of the R & R Royal Treatment Salon. Chandler had several beauty parlors, but surely there were enough women in the city that a new hairdresser could make a go of it. As I opened the door the fruity fragrance of shampoo, conditioner, and hairspray assailed me. The Royal Treatment was a three-chair salon. Two of the chairs were occupied by young women in black smocks filing their fingernails. They both jumped out of the chairs as I entered.

"May we help you?" one asked.

I laughed. "You undoubtedly could, but today I am on a mission."

"Oh." The inflection in her tone went down a notch.

I did believe she was disappointed that I had not come in for service. I introduced myself and the purpose of my call.

". . . and our next breakfast meeting will be at 7:00 on Tuesday."

"Well, we are Rachel and Rebecca, the R & R of the Royal Treatment Salon. For six years we worked at Andre's in Phoenix. We pooled our resources and with the help of Rachel's dad we set up a shop of our own."

I looked around the new establishment, clean and neat and modestly furnished. Framed posters of models sporting extravagant hair styles decorated the walls. A couple of hair style magazines lay on a small table in the waiting area. The magazines had not achieved the dog-eared thumbed-through look of magazines in more established parlors. The shelf behind the receptionist counter contained a small selection of shampoos, sprays, and tonics. A hand-lettered sign on white marker board listed a full battery of cosmetology services available at the R & R. A hair wash sink and a couple of dryers completed the accoutrements.

Rachel and Rebecca were open for business and now they needed customers.

"If you come to our meeting you can tell the group about your services," I said. "I'll be glad to arrange for you to be on the agenda. In fact, if you have business cards or flyers you could distribute those, too."

By now, the girls had warmed up to me. "So you own the stationery store. Do you have a copy machine? We'll need to make some flyers."

"Why, yes, we have a copy machine. If you need to make flyers, the first fifty will be on the house."

"We're so glad you came," Rebecca (or was she Rachel?) said. She reached into a drawer at the receptionist station and pulled out a small card. "We want you to be a member of our haircut club."

"Each time you get a haircut here we will punch this card." Rachel (or was she Rebecca?) took over.

"After seven punches we'll give you a free cut." Rebecca (or was she Rachel?) punched the first notch on the card and handed it to me. "The first punch is on the house," she said

"The haircut club," I chuckled. "I'll be glad to join, as long as I don't have to be secretary.

Chapter 36

HANKY PANKY

For weeks the windows of the old building had been covered with brown craft paper. Construction trucks and maintenance vehicles pulled up to the curb and a parade of carpenters, painters, electricians, plumbers, glaziers, and tile setters paraded in and out the front door.

"What's going on at the old Granillo's?" I asked.

"I heard that the building's owner finally leased the space," Arnold, the barber, replied.

The building had been vacant for months, ever since the Granillos closed their clothing store. In the ensuing months paper napkins and Big Gulp cups collected in the doorway. Beyond cracked fly-specked windows yawned a dusty cavern littered with broken shelves and empty display racks, ghosts of the family emporium.

"That's good. It takes longer and longer to fill empty stores."

"The new tenants are not wasting any time refurbishing the place," Arnold continued.

Located on the southeast corner of Arizona and Boston Avenues, the building commanded a prime retail spot on the square. It would take a business of some means to occupy the space of this abandoned site.

"Too bad the fashion outlet didn't work out," I mused. "Who is the new tenant?"

"I haven't heard," Arnold answered

At one time rumor had it that a fashion outlet would

rent the space. Large plate-glass windows spanning the front of the store provided a perfect setting for trendy mannequins. Alas, the fashion outlet never materialized. Then we heard that a sporting goods store was interested. Wouldn't that be fine? A local vendor to supply Little League and Pop Warner teams with their equipment. These deals, also, never got off the drawing board.

A diner rejected the site because it would be too expensive to install a kitchen and bring utilities up to code. The bereft building was also rejected by an antique store, a music store, and an appliance center.

"Well, a surge of new life is unfolding before our eyes," I continued.

"Strange that the proprietor of the building hasn't kept us informed of the status of his new tenant." Arnold returned to his Clip Joint next door.

Merchandise began arriving at the door of the new business on the square. An endless stream of crates and cardboard cartons were wheeled into the maw. The shopkeeper and his employees were obviously very busy unpacking and displaying the contents of the parcels. The front door was never open for curious neighbors to step in and introduce themselves.

"There's a lot going on across the street, but I haven't met a single person connected to the new store." Arnold was back, and we continued our speculations about the new store on the square.

"I guess it's wait and see," was all I had to say.

The last time the store fronts around the square had been remodeled shopkeepers were restricted to a predetermined color pallet and guidelines for signage. The new business on the block was carefully adhering to the established code. Now the name of the business was being installed over the colonnade. In fifteen-inch Broadway letters.

"Hanky Panky?" I puzzled. "That sounds a bit racy."

Hanky Panky was the new store on the block.

Hanky Panky! An adult trinket shop was in our midst! A sex shop! Lingerie, books, games, and paraphernalia with a decided spin toward hanky panky would be the product at hand!

The craft paper was peeled from the display windows and cleverly arranged mannequins in wispy bikinis strutted their stuff. Boots and bras, leather and lace, masks and manacles!

"Oh, my goodness!" I gasped. I stole a furtive glance in the window as I passed Hanky Panky on an improvised errand to the city buildings on the other side of the square.

The Downtown Merchants' Association was set on its heels. As was the custom of the association, the owner of a new establishment on the square was invited to a monthly breakfast meeting to tell us about his business and then was encouraged to join the group.

A well-heeled businessman in a pin-striped suit represented Hanky Panky. He seemed unaffected by the chilly atmosphere in the room; he apparently was accustomed to operating in hostile environments. When called upon to speak about his business Mr. Hanky Panky droned on about the overall demand for his business, the discretion of his business, and rights given by the First Amendment.

"Privacy and anonymity are our keystones," Mr. Hanky Panky informed us. "We will have a back door entrance for customers who prefer not to enter from the front.

"We have complied with all city zoning ordinances," Mr. Hanky Panky continued. "We are located more than 500 feet from any school, church, or residential property."

Most of us sat in stony silence while we listened. A few barbed comments were thrown to him.

"A sex shop invites the work of the devil into a community," the jeweler proclaimed.

"It is the first step to a prostitute operation," said the florist.

"We can expect an upsurge of crime," said an

insurance agent.

"And a decline in property values," from a real estate broker.

"Stores like yours will attract perverts to a quaint business district," said the owner of the coffee shop that was located next door to the controversial establishment.

"There is no evidence that any of your concerns are valid," Mr. Hanky Panky countered. "We will be a 60-40 operation. In other words sixty percent of our merchandise will be mainstream product. No more than forty percent will be devoted to erotica and that will be segregated in the back half of the store. On the surface we won't appear any different from Frederick's of Hollywood that is in every shopping mall in the country."

He assured us that minors would not be permitted in the establishment and that the building would be well-maintained.

It was a done-deal. Hanky Panky was on the square and open for trade. The man had a proper business permit, a tax license, and had adhered to all city codes. That was the only meeting of the Downtown Merchants' Association that Mr. Hanky Panky attended. He was not pressed to join the group. Nor did he ask.

"I never see customers come out of the Hanky Panky with shopping bags," I said to Arnold. I slipped his purchase of a box of ballpoint pens into one of our merchandise bags. I was thinking of stores around the square that had personalized bags advertising where shoppers had taken their patronage. "For that matter, I never see anyone go into the Hanky Panky."

"There is a discrete back-door entrance," Arnold replied. "You aren't supposed to know who shops at the Hanky Panky. Besides, they package their product in plain brown paper tied with string."

"Humpf," I snorted. *Brown paper packages tied up with string. Seems like a nefarious operation.*

"And," continued Arnold, "they're open from 11:00 a.m. 'til 2:00 a.m. Most of their business is done long after you close."

And what else does Arnold know about the Hanky Panky that I don't?

"Well, that makes them conveniently poised for Luigi's 1:00 a.m. revelers," I responded.

Arnold paid for his pens and returned to the barbershop.

Time passed in strained harmony. The Hanky Panky kept its sidewalk swept and its door knobs polished. Bambi, Binki and Bridget (the front window mannequins) paraded behind shiny glass windows in bare essentials, perhaps not X-rated, but certainly suggestive. Sometimes they sported boas and fish net hose. Sometimes they twirled ropes. Sometimes they dangled chains. The displays changed regularly, so there was always an astonishing view on stage.

The Hanky Panky even brought a bit of trade our way. Occasionally Mr. Hanky Panky or one of his sales girls came into Chandler Stationers to purchase a ledger or a package of sales books – bare essentials of running a retail store. The Hanky Panky method of keeping business records seemed to be like that of any other store. They never opened a charge account with us or wrote a check; transactions were always cash and carry.

Because my proclivities did not tend toward the products Hanky Panky promoted, I did not return the patronage. However, I did acquire a "live and let live" attitude.

Late one afternoon Big Red Allenspach lumbered into the store. He settled in front of the anniversary cards ultimately selecting the biggest and floweriest card in the rack for his wife. Wife-number-four had lasted nigh-on twenty years.

"Put this on the agency account," he said tossing the

card on the counter.

At that moment a parcel slipped from under his arm and fell to the floor. A brown paper package tied up with string.

Hanky Panky had infiltrated the ranks.

Chapter 37

NOT WITHOUT A FIGHT

"We won't go down without a fight."

I sat across from Dad at the Whoppin' Burger. He was attempting to scrape off the secret sauce that oozed between slices of sesame bun. A mélange of catsup, mayo, and anonymous ingredients dribbled through his fingers and began to roll down his arm. Then the whole thing collapsed – a landslide of shredded lettuce, tomatoes, onions, and pickles. Dad flung his ill-advised lunch choice down on the plastic tray.

"Twenty-five years and these haven't gotten any better," he growled.

I had been on an errand between the Chandler and Phoenix stores when Dad asked me to join him at the next-door burger joint for a bite to eat. I knew he hadn't invited me for the cuisine.

He didn't miss my cocked eyebrow. My unspoken "Why do you order these things?" hung in the air.

"Well, they are customers," he feebly protested. "I have to buy a hamburger every now and then."

"Maybe you should stick to their stale coffee." I pushed my Styrofoam cup of black sludge away.

"We won't go down without a fight," Dad repeated, and brought me back to the realization we had come to the Whoppin' Burger to talk, not to eat.

"Who would have guessed this trend when we entered the office supply business?" Dad continued. "Stationery stores were thriving little businesses. We've had a good run."

I knew then Dad was referring to the influx of Mega Office Supply Stores that were springing up throughout the valley. In fact one MOSS had opened its doors not a mile from our Indian School location.

"I've checked them out," Dad continued. "Their basic prices throughout the store are the same as ours. We've always priced our product according to the manufacturers' suggested retail. They do the same. We have a greater depth of inventory and a greater variety of product. Their advantage is flashy advertising and loss leaders that bring customers into their stores. . . . and they carry more computer gizmos."

Dad was referring to floppy discs, cables, modems, monitors, and dot matrix printers. Beyond opening our stores to fax and Xerox machines Dad had not concerned himself with the impending electronic revolution. We were the A to Z of office supplies, our catalog an inch thick. A lot of product filled the pages between its covers – from Acco Binders to Zip Code Directories

"I know," I said. "Just this morning I saw a MOSS advertising insert in the *Republic*. They are advertising cases of copy paper for $19.99. How can they sell paper at that price?"

Advertising was always the bane for small businesses. Newspaper, radio/television, and direct mail ads were enormously expensive. Chandler Stationers/Indian School Stationers had thrown their advertising dollars into an imposing half-page ad in the Metropolitan Phoenix phone book. When a potential customer needed a particular product he referred to the Yellow Pages. And we were prominent among office supply stores having cross-references to services we offered.

"Paper prices are at the mercy of the timber industry." Dad answered my question. "Paper prices have gone up exponentially in recent years. We have to charge at least eight dollars more a case. The MOSS stores can't hold the price of $19.99 for long."

In the years that we had been in business we had seen corner grocery stores succumb to the influx of out-of-state supermarkets. Local diners had been run out of business by Super Burgers. Independent hardware stores yielded to Home Improvement Capitals.

I was convinced this was a calculated conspiracy. Earlier in the spring I sat behind a couple of yuppies on an airplane flight between Kansas City and Phoenix. They were regaling the stewardess (yes, stewardess) that they represented a major burger chain. They'd just set up a fast-food Mecca in small-town Kansas. They bragged that the chain would advertise burgers for low-low prices and hand out coupons for free kids' meals. They planned to run the local mom and pop diners out of business and then raise their prices. To this day I cannot choke down a hamburger from that chain.

The current target seemed to be the office supply stores.

"We have to regroup," Dad continued. "We won't go down without a fight."

* * *

I saw Dad again the next morning. Hooked up to tubes and drips and drains in the emergency room at St Joseph's Hospital he now fought a different battle. Needles and wires led to tanks and machines that beeped and blinked maniacally. Rows of etch-a-sketch lines darted across computer screens, a jagged trail of spikes and dips.

Around me people moaned and wheezed, grunted and cried. Hospital staff scurried about in color-coded scrubs, stethoscopes dangling about their necks, rubber-soled shoes squeaking against the floor tiles. They carried clipboards, IV bags, syringes, and gauze bandages. The hospital intercom barked emergency codes. Phones rang; keyboards clicked; wheelchairs whirred.

Dad had suffered a devastating cerebral aneurysm during the night. Hours had passed before emergency crews were called and he was transported to the hospital. At the point I arrived on the scene doctors were still sorting all of this out.

His head swollen to the size of a basketball, his face mottled with bruises caused by blood draining from the burst artery, Dad, a man who avoided doctors at all costs, was now at the mercy of the medical community.

As I paced the waiting room floor hospital smells wafted through the halls: disinfectants and antiseptic cleansers from housekeeping carts; meatballs, fish, and soup from cafeteria trays; roses and carnations from floral bouquets.

Emergency surgery. Stents. Tubes. Drains.

Days turned into weeks turned into . . .

Through the ordeal Mother diminished before my eyes to the point of becoming irrational.

"Mother, let's go to the store and sort through Dad's desk. We need to see what he was working on."

"Not now. I'll take care of that later."

"Mother, Westcom hasn't been paid for the filing cabinets that came last month."

"I'll send a check when I get to the office."

"Mother, payroll is due tomorrow."

"Payroll can wait."

"Susan, you have to get your mother to let you step up to the plate." Jeff was now fielding dunning notices from suppliers. "Unified Office Products will cut us off if we don't keep our account current."

"Mother is scared," I said. But the fact was that I had never been in the unenviable position of having to buck my mother.

We won't go down without a fight.

The fight had taken a new direction.

Amazingly, after months of therapy, Dad rallied somewhat. He relearned to walk, to talk, to feed himself, and to dress himself. He was released from the hospital on his 80th birthday; however, he was but a shell of his former self.

* * *

Meanwhile back at the store. My brother Bill, Jr. took a hiatus from his construction work in Wyoming and stepped into the Indian School store ostensibly to help Mother and Dad. His manner of running a stationery store was akin to bulldozing fog – ineffective against Dad's confusion and Mother's passive resistance to dealing with necessary issues.

Dad marginally improved; Mother, on the other hand, began a gradual decline into the dark world of Alzheimer's.

During this period Bill, Jr. and I began the painful task of untangling business and family finances, of reorganizing the store hierarchy so that he became owner/operator of the Indian School store and I became owner/operator of the Chandler store.

* * *

Stalwart Jeff watched the fracture of a family business with helpless dismay. He began to explore career opportunities in a burgeoning field that had not been in the curriculum when he was in college – ecology.

As a result of environmental impact laws, before any construction project could commence, an environmental survey had to be taken. If endangered plants or animals were in the path of such a project, strict monitoring was part of the plan.

Because of his university degrees, his strong biology background, and his knowledge of Arizona flora and fauna, Jeff was properly accredited for much of this survey work. He accepted an occasional job as consultant and field biologist along highway and bridge construction routes, along power lines and pipelines crossing the state. He pulled his hiking boots out of the closet, his slouchy field hat, and his multi-pocketed vest. Armed with backpack, binoculars, bird calls, topo maps, field notebooks, and camera Jeff was back in his element traipsing over the back country.

While Jeff was on-again, off-again at the store, I held things together by a thread. When he was out in the field our paths crossed on weekends. He stopped in to mow the lawn, and get a fresh set of clothes for the next week. And I dashed into Phoenix to check on my parents, deliver a casserole, toss their sheets in the laundry, and put a week's accumulation of dirty dishes in the dishwasher.

One evening Jeff rubbed my head gently, the same endearing stroke he gave old Pooch who had served faithfully until his end was near. "I'm submitting my resignation," he said.

At this point the fight became mine.

Chapter 38

DO SOMETHING . . . EVEN IF IT'S WRONG

"Do something. Even if it's wrong." I could hear Dad admonishing us from his grave. "If you've never done anything wrong, you've never done anything."

My brother and I, having received our tattered inheritances early, began operating the Indian School Store and the Chandler Store as separate but co-operative entities. We functioned like this for five years. And during those years we buried our parents.

One evening I was browsing in a mall bookstore. Since my favorite Book Nook had closed several years earlier, even *I* had resorted to patronizing big-box bookstores. *Ten Easy Steps to Staying in Business* jumped out at me from the shelves. Ten-easy-steps sounded doable. I had high hopes that with the $12.95 book investment I would gain fresh insight into operating a store profitably.

A week passed before I had the time or energy to crack the little tome. My customary routine upon locking the store for the night was to drag home a briefcase bulging with ledgers to balance, invoices to pay, and catalogs to generate orders. I couldn't seem to find time to do these critical tasks during store hours. A quick dinner and a late session with the work I brought home consumed most evenings.

But one evening my load was not so heavy. I warmed a cup of left-over soup in the microwave and stood at the counter eating my dinner as I watched the evening news. I rinsed out my soup cup and headed to the bedroom for a coveted early retirement. *Ten Easy Steps to Staying in Business* winked at me from the bedside table. *Time to get on the stick and find out how easy it is to stay in business.* I fluffed my pillows against the headboard and crawled into bed, book in hand.

I began leafing through the chapters. The lessons in the book were thirty years late in coming.

Chapter 1. "Create a Life Plan." *Plan your life, and then plan your business.* "Balderdash!" Dad said from the grave. "My life plan was to work. If I hadn't been struck by a damned aneurysm, I would've died in my brown suede brogues pacing the aisles of the stationery store."

Ten easy steps to staying in business

Chapter 2. "Choose a Business Model." *Select a business model that reflects your life plan.* "Eh? This is double-speak?" Again Dad's voice from the grave. "There's nothing to choose. We're a brick-and-mortar operation on a little town square."

Chapter 3. "Formulate a Business Plan." *A business plan details your life plan and your business model.* "Poppycock!" Dad again. "The whole plan is to sell office products and make a bit of profit to boot."

Chapter 4. "Determine a Business Structure." *It is*

important to view your life plan and your business plan to determine the legal structure of your business. "Bosh! They're talking in circles!" Dad's voice exploded in my head. "Without a life plan or a business plan we managed to organize as a corporate entity."

I was ready to throw the *Ten Easy Steps to Staying in Business* in the trash when I came to Chapter Five. Maybe this chapter had some merit.

Chapter 5. "Find Key People." *The single most important factor in the success of a company is its employees.* "You have key people under your nose," Dad admonished.

I had a small but loyal staff that seemed supportive of my attempts to keep the business on track. But key employees? Employees that would pick up the torch and carry it to the next level? Not likely. My employees were, at a minimum, ten years my senior.

I thought of my daughters. Good workers, they were. They helped out in the store on an "as needed" basis when their own busy lives allowed. Heather was beginning a Master's program in Spanish Literature at the University of Arizona. She was seldom in town. Beth, following in her father's footsteps, was working in an environmental consulting firm. Katie was in a drafting program at the local community college.

Any mention of store ownership . . . "One of these days, this can be yours . . ." and their eyes glazed over. There was no hope in the next generation of my family stepping into the family store.

This was a moment of realization for me. Chandler Stationers was my baby. I could give it my best shot to stay afloat. I could institute some of my own ideas into products and policies we adopted. Most important, I could have fun in the process. No matter what happened, I was empowered.

I hurled *Ten Easy Steps to Staying in Business* across the room, rolled over and went to sleep.

Chapter 39

ONE GIANT LEAP FOR MANKIND

Front page news. Neil Armstrong is dead.

As I pen my memories of nigh-on forty years I am struck by how singularly this man's historic mission touched our lives and our careers.

Armstrong's name spiraled to fame on July 20, 1969 when he became the first human to set foot upon the Moon. He was spacecraft commander for Apollo 11, the first manned lunar landing mission.

As he stepped off the lunar module onto the powdery surface of the moon Armstrong's proclamation echoed round the world. "That's one small step for man, one giant leap for mankind."

I had gathered my little girls – Heather was but four years old and Beth not even a year – to sit on the floor in front of our old black-and-white screen Magnavox and watch the momentous event. Until then "the cow jumped over the moon" was the extent of my children's exposure to space travel. I wanted them to witness the historic moment, to be able to say later, "I saw the first man to walk on the moon."

An adventure rivaling the escapades of Buck Rogers and Flash Gordon unfolded before our eyes. The moon walk culminated a program that not only launched man into orbit around the earth, but spun him to a destination 240,000 miles beyond the horizon. Grainy images flitted across the screen – the stuff of science fiction, of other worlds, of exotic kingdoms and distant galaxies.

I had just stepped into the office supply business and was learning the ins-and-outs of bookkeeping systems, typewriter ribbons, filing equipment, writing instruments, and drafting tools. Some of the very basics, so integral to office operation at that time, were rendered obsolete during the course of the space program, and a number of new office products came about or spiraled to prominence.

When I was in college I took my class notes with a fine-point Esterbrook fountain pen. I filled the margins of *The Complete Works of Shakespeare* with cryptic comments scribbled in blue ink. My spidery lines went on to underline profound passages in *Hamlet*. I did not use a ballpoint pen. Ballpoints of that era skipped, leaked, and often failed to write. Because of complaints, the ballpoint died a consumer death.

By the time that I was in the office supply business, ballpoint pens had made an anemic resurgence, and the old standard brands lined the pen shelf: Bic, Koh-i-Noor, Lindy, Papermate, Parker. But, even the stalwarts occasionally succumbed to lesser standards of writing.

Astronauts, however, needed a foil-proof writing instrument. They needed a pen that would write in conditions experienced during spaceflight. NASA spent a large amount of money to develop a pen that would write at any angle, underwater, over wet and greasy paper, and in very hot and very cold environments. The Space Pen, also known as the Zero Gravity Pen, answered all the requirements. This marvel of the space age became available to the man on the street and was sold in stationery stores.

"One small *click* for man."

The space suit that Neil Armstrong wore on his moon walk promoted another space product to the world at large, Velcro. The bulky white snow-suit-like garment designed to keep a man alive in the harsh environment of outer space was augmented by complex systems involving oxygen, pressure, temperature, radiation, ventilation, and communication. The space suit had a plethora of hoses, belts, tabs, hooks, and lanyards. NASA quickly recognized the value of a sticky hook and loop strip called Velcro as a closure and fastening device for the many parts of the cumbersome suit. Velcro also anchored equipment so that it did not float around in space.

Earth-side Velcro appeared as fasteners to sports clothing; then it spiraled into a myriad of uses for medicine, industry, and home. For the office Velcro came into its own as a method of bundling electronic cords, adhering charts to walls, hanging pictures, and organizing keys. Velcro secured pencils to telephones, pens to notebooks, markers to communication boards. Backpacks, briefcases, and portfolios were likely to have Velcro closures. There was no excuse for not keeping it together with Velcro on hand.

"One small *grip* for man."

When Neil Armstrong set foot on the moon another milestone for man occurred. The legendary Apollo 11 mission landed a laser reflector on the moon's surface. A laser device emits a very intense beam of light. The reflector set on the moon in 1969 measured the exact distance between Earth and its orbit. Laser technology quickly spread to uses in medicine, industry, entertainment, and commerce. Laser printers and laser bar code readers became the norm in retail businesses.

In the mundane office supply business the laser pointer went on the shelves. In the past teachers, professors, salesmen, and public speakers wielded long tapered sticks called pointers when they were making presentations. I recall an art history professor in college whopping his pointer across the screen as slides of the Acropolis drifted across. Then he proceeded to tap, none too gently, a football player who had fallen asleep during the dreary presentation.

The laser pointer, in contrast, was a small pen-like instrument that a teacher could carry in his pocket. With the click of a switch he could transmit a beam of light to the point on the chart or graph or picture that he was emphasizing. No more tickling a recalcitrant student with a rod.

"One small *beam* for man."

Teflon, that wonder product that keeps your waffles from sticking to your waffle iron was actually in use years before the space program. It had earned acclaim in another government venture called The Manhattan Project, a research program that produced the first atomic bomb. However, Teflon came to the attention of the rest of the world during the space program with far less devastating consequences. The Apollo moon shot mission used Teflon in the construction of space suits, to coat surfaces of moving parts of the module, and as insulation for electric cables. It arrived at the office in the form of Teflon tape and non-stick scissors, "One small *glide* for man."

Even that jar of Tang that sat on the shelf in the break room gained its popularity in the space age. Astronauts needed nutritious food that was easy and safe to store and could be prepared under the constraints of space travel. Add water and stir. The convenience of freeze dried food was picked up by outdoor enthusiasts, hikers, campers, back packers and then by commuters and the office world. Those small cups of freeze-dried soup to which I added water and cooked in the microwave for lunch could be attributed to the space program.

"One small *taste* for man."

Computers, cell phones, fax machines, GPS systems, unheard of (or in their infancy) when we went into business, blossomed during the space age and came to dictate trends in office products. Office furniture was redesigned to accommodate towers, monitors, keyboards, and printers. Into our inventory went floppy discs, cables, storage systems, printer cartridges, and mouse pads. Mouse pads! Eek!

Weren't they ingenious devices for trapping rodents!

My little girls grew up as the space age unfolded. Today they communicate via iPad, iPod, iPhone, eMail; their vocabulary encompasses alphabetic gibberish PC CD DVD, GPS, MP3, USB, VCR, ROM, SIMS. Of course they do not remember Neil Armstrong's famous moon walk and probably don't realize the domino effect it had on our business and our lives.

I can only speculate what our lives would have been had Neil Armstrong not made "one giant leap for mankind."

Chapter 40

AFTER THIRTY YEARS

Every afternoon about 3:00 I sequestered myself in the office. That is, if a mild crisis did not detain me. Yesterday five firemen trooped in at precisely 3:00 to perform their annual inspection of the premise. They issued a citation because our fire extinguishers were past due to be recharged. I couldn't seem to stay on top of that once-a-year task. *To do: Call Allied Fire Equipment.*

The day before, a flock of Chandler High School students inundated us after school. They needed compasses and protractors for math. We did not have enough in stock. Why didn't the teacher let us know he would be sending twenty kids to our store for economical models of these instruments? *To do: Order two dozen compasses and protractors.*

This afternoon, before I could escape to my lair, I found myself dealing with crotchety old Miss Higgins who complained about a list finder that she purchased last month. Precursor to computerized address systems this handy-dandy metal telephone directory had a gliding selector that moved along the index. When the selector reached a desired letter of the alphabet, the touch of a finger popped the directory open. The problem was that when Miss Higgins pressed "C" to get Cynthia Carter's telephone number, the "D" listing came into view. And so it went through the alphabet; the "slidomatic" selector was one letter off. *Hmmm.* A noticeable ding on the right bottom corner of the product suggested that it had been knocked off a desk and met misfortune on a hard floor. Oh well, Miss Higgins was an old customer. *To do: Give Miss Higgins another list finder.*

It was already 3:25. I scurried down the middle aisle. A vast array of pens and pencils, ink and erasers, rulers, scissors, clips, glue, and tape lined the shelves.

I should be able to get the deposit finalized and to the bank before it closed at 4:00. I shut the office door then pulled yesterday's money bag from a locked cabinet. I still had to tally a stack of checks. *Why hadn't I done this earlier in the day?*

I inserted a sheet of carbon paper between two deposit slips. I needed to keep a copy of the bank transaction in my files. Then I rolled the forms through the carriage of my classic Smith Corona. *Clickity click . . . tab . . . click click . . . zing. Clickity click . . . tab . . . click click . . . zing.*

With scant minutes to spare I zipped the deposit bag and headed for the front door. Giving a cursory nod to Lillian who was attending the cash register I let her know I was leaving. Fortunately, Valley National Bank was on the corner of the block. With luck I would slip into the bank foyer before its doors were locked.

Because I was under the gun for time I made a beeline to the bank. I did not wave to my fellow merchants as I bustled past their doors. Balmy February in Central Arizona allowed them to open their portals to the trade, a welcome contrast to blistering summer months when triple digit temperatures forced them to conduct business in air conditioned isolation behind closed doors.

The half-block walk to the bank reminded me that there had been many changes on the plaza during the past thirty years. Stores had come and gone. Proprietors had changed. Yet much was amazingly the same.

Whiffs of my neighbors' trades and fragments of conversation trailed me down the block. The scent of talcum and aftershave wafted from The Clip Joint next door. A classic red and white striped barber pole stood sentry at the door. *"How 'bout them Brewers. . ."* Arnold was undoubtedly ranting about a spring training baseball game at Compadre Stadium, Chandler's nod to the minor leagues.

As I passed the Kountry Kitchen the heady aroma of strong fresh coffee reminded me that my energy was flagging. Maude always put a fresh pot of coffee on the burners for the spit-and-whittle club that convened mid-afternoon in the front corner booth. These were the community philosophers. *"Until there's a complete change on the city council, this city will never . . ."* The Kountry Kitchen was a breakfast and lunch establishment. Maude would pull the shades and lock the doors as soon as the guys left and she had finished mopping her floor.

Leather and saddle soap were trademark scents of the Pecos Bootery. I could see Slim at his work station hunched over a shoe form and surrounded by glue pots and stitchery devices. Slim Jim Owens had taken over the trade after an uncle died. His shop was not much for presentation. Dusty saddles were featured in his fly-speckled show window. On the shelves behind the counter scuffed boots sporting new heels and soles formed a pigeon-toed parade waiting to be claimed by cowboys, hikers, farm workers, and electricians.

The distinctive aromas of ammonia and hair spray assailed me as I passed Hannah's House of Hair. Hannah subtly catered to the mature woman. You didn't see extreme cuts or exotic colors walking out her door. The younger set seemed to gravitate to Cassandra's on the north edge of town. A matron swathed in a purple plastic cape, one side of her hair coiled in pink rods was regaling Hannah *". . . and then she said . . ."*

The Nile Theater had been located next to Valley National Bank for decades. When the old theater closed, the building was gutted, and then sat vacant for several years. What could you do with a defunct movie theater? And then Lionel and Roland moved in. They were a rather clever duo. With a can of mauve paint they visually transformed the old lobby, and then introduced an eclectic assortment of antiques, gifts, handcrafts, and art. Scented candles and smoldering incense contributed an aura of mystique to a shop that had no window display. Today an old steamer trunk stood outside the door to lure shoppers into the inner sanctum, an arrangement of kid gloves, lace hankies, plumed hats, and high button shoes artistically displayed in its open drawers.

At the north corner of the block stood Valley National Bank, an old Arizona institution, VNB dated back to pre-statehood days, which meant it was organized about the turn of the 20th Century. VNB branches were located in almost every Podunk town in Arizona. A major anchor on the square at the corner of Buffalo Street and San Marcos Place, the Chandler branch smacked of remodeled 1950s architecture. A recessed flank of dark plate glass windows formed the front wall facing the sidewalk.

In the ensuing years I had become my mother.

I turned toward the bank's entrance, a chrome and glass door at the north end of the wall. From the door, a portly woman approached me. A worrisome frown creased her brow. She straightened her shoulders and tried to suck in her tummy. She clutched the lapels of her drab grey jacket pulling them over a coffee spot on the front of her blouse. Her scuffed shoes, worn down at the heels, might have profited from a recapping job at the bootery. Her lackluster hair, beginning to grey at the temples, would have benefited from an afternoon at Hannah's House of Hair.

"Mother!" I whispered.

I shook my head in momentary confusion. Mother was gone. She had spent her last years in agitated befuddlement before succumbing to the ravages of Alzheimer's. She had been laid to rest with Dad in the Veterans Memorial Cemetery. Recently enough that the pain was still sharp.

I again shook my head as I came to my senses. My own reflection had greeted me as I approached the bank door. In the ensuing years, I had become my mother.

Chapter 41

DEAR DIARY

July

Summer rains were on the horizon. Not that Central Arizona has a long and dreary rainy season, but our summer monsoon storms are often preceded by fierce wind and dust. Microbursts, like small tornados, can cause severe localized damage.

In the past several years infrequent cloudbursts had exposed a small leak in the roof near the back door of the store. We skirted the roof repair issue by setting a coffee can on the floor where drops fell from the ceiling.

Jeff had performed occasional patches on the roof in the past. The repairs held for a short time, but since I had been running the store no one had set foot on the roof. As long as the sun shone, roof repairs were low priority. And the sun shone most of the time in Central Arizona. The coffee can had done a commendable job of catching the few splats that made their way through the rafters.

On this July afternoon, thunder clouds roiled in from the southeast. Lightning popped over the San Tan Mountains. An ominous tower of dust surged over the valley. I was anxious to get home before the eye of the storm struck. However, before I closed the store for the evening I took the precaution of setting a coffee can under the precarious spot in the stockroom.

Winds hit. Tree branches cracked. Garbage cans toppled. In my ten-mile trip home, major street lights went out. Rain began pelting in solid sheets, and water ran curb to curb in the streets. I arrived home to a dark house where I hunkered down until electricity was restored a couple of hours later.

Summer storms were not usually long-lasting. By morning the sun gleamed innocently, as if the torrent of the night before was merely a little joke.

When I arrived at the store, I found that the tempest had centered over Chandler Stationers. It tore into the fragile roof on the north side of the store, peeled the tarpaper and soaked the plaster. The valiant coffee can had lost its battle against the elements; it overflowed and rivulets of water trickled through the aisles of the stockroom. In the main showroom a fault line in the ceiling running the length of our greeting card racks cracked open to admit a deluge that soaked the cards. Tubs of gift wrap bows floated in their own little lakes. Over the fine gifts the roof had leaked like a sieve. Crystal compotes and china teacups were filled with murky residue. Dresden figurines were up to their lace pantaloons in puddles of water.

August

The Devil settled into Central Arizona and commenced to making his summer playground as hot as Hell. His torrid breath nudged daytime temperatures to 118°. He tampered with water lines so that scalding water spewed from both hot and cold taps. He turned diabolic flames under the city streets reducing them to molten slag. When I went to the post office at noon I burned my hand opening the car door; then I navigated a half-mile to the post office using but the tips of two fingers on the blistering steering wheel.

But the Devil was not yet finished with his demonic pranks. The fiend turned his malice toward Chandler Stationers. He tweaked electronic circuits on our air conditioning system. Temperatures inside the building soared to infernal highs. A burnt out compressor, Orville's AC informed me. I'd need a new unit. If this misfortune had happened in September I might have tried to cobble through the season with one unit working on the north side of the store.

But, in August, I'd have to bite the bullet and install a new unit. If I didn't have a comfortable store for shopping, I wouldn't have any customers.

And the Devil winked.

September

Oh my gosh! Four hundred dollars! The little employees' bathroom, a one-toilet one-sink convenience, could not possibly generate a four hundred dollar water bill. The Devil had played a final trick before returning to Hades. He tore a hole in a water pipe near the main conduit in the alley creating an underground lake behind the store.

The Devil tipped his hat and said, "I have done my job."

October

Several gremlins descended upon the store before closing time. Melinda Wilkins had brought with her a pirate, a scarecrow, a princess, a clown, and three indeterminate ghouls. Whoa! That was more children than I remembered in the Wilkins family. I guessed Melinda was taking the neighbor kids trick-or-treating after she finished her errand at the store. I opened a package of Halloween stickers and gave each trick-or-treater a page of jack-o-lanterns and black cats thus averting soaped windows.

I locked the door, dealt with the closing-out routine of the store, and then gathered some record books to take home with me. The last day of the month and I had other bogeymen to face.

I spent the evening balancing the checkbook and ledgers. I'd better not deposit my paychecks next month.

November

Black Friday, the day after Thanksgiving, was the

customary kick-off to the Christmas season. Like many merchants who operated marginally or "in the red" from January through November, we counted on Black Friday to turn the tides of our business and put us "in the black."

Friday morning was woefully slow. Frenetic shoppers were following glitzy ads to department stores in the malls that opened at five in the morning to accommodate holiday whimsies.

By mid-afternoon, disgruntled shoppers began drifting into Chandler Stationers. They had found the mall stores crowded, clerks untrained, and parking places non-existent. Not only that, after standing in line for two hours to purchase a Super Nintendo or an Easy Bake Oven, shoppers discovered that many coveted items had sold out.

Perhaps the local merchant had something to offer after all.

December

Holiday music tinkles in the background. Lights are low. Mistletoe hangs from chandeliers in artistic sprays. Gorgeous ladies in slinky black dresses nibble on fish-egg canapés. Suave gentlemen swirl glasses filled with amber potions. Undercurrents of mystery fill the air. From this sultry setting the reader know that something electrifying is about to happen. In the realm of romance novels, this is the company Christmas party.

We locked the door on Christmas Eve. Now was the time for our company holiday celebration. Shelves were askew; a garland of tinsel had come untacked from over the counter and dangled morosely to the floor. I removed the drawer from the cash register and headed to the office to lock it away. The tinsel caught on my shoe and followed me down the aisle leaving a glittery trail.

The clerks met me in the stockroom. I pushed up the sleeves of my Santa sweater to begin Christmas hospitalities. Santa looked a bit forlorn, his flocked beard frayed, the sequins covering his hat tarnished.

A platter of holiday cookies and fruitcake that I had set on the gift-wrap counter in the morning had been picked over. The yummy seven-layer bars were all gone as were the lemon snaps. No one had touched the fruitcake. I apparently couldn't pass off the glazed confection that a salesman had left on my desk early in the season.

I opened the refrigerator and pulled out a bottle of champagne – a $3.98 special that I had picked up at Osco Drug Store on the way to work. I managed to create a volcanic eruption as the cork I struggled with shot out of the bottle. The characteristic crackling and fizzing of the effervescent beverage was somewhat muted as I poured it into Frosty the Snowman paper cups. I made a simple toast and distributed the year's bonus checks.

"Merry Christmas to all!"

January

Time to negotiate a new lease. The old building that we leased was part of the historic Price Estate that owned several properties on the square. The lease had always been amenable to both parties. Any maintenance, construction, or repairs inside the building was the responsibility of the lessee (us). Thus, lowering the ceiling, new paint, new floor tile, windows, and yes, the air conditioners fell on our side of the balance. Structural repairs and maintenance outside the building were responsibilities of the lessor (the Price Estate). Thus, repairs following the plumbing and roofing disasters became obligations of the lessor. We, never-the-less, were responsible for the water bill and the damage inside the building as a result of the roof leak.

For over thirty years we had sent rent checks to an impersonal bank account in Phoenix. Every five years a lease renewal arrived in the mail. The conditions of the lease remained static, with the exception of a clause that included allowable escalations in the rent.

I had to decide if I would accept the terms of the lease.

Chapter 42

FIFTEEN MINUTES OF FAME

Customers began trickling in, goldenrod flyers in hand. I had timed the mailing to arrive the day that notice hit the newspaper and signs went up in the windows.

Chandler Stationers will close March 31.

Celebrate with us. Stop in and say goodbye. We are unearthing 65 years worth of product and memories of doing business in Chandler (over 30 years under current ownership).

Week One:

"I am not happy at all," wailed Bernice Kelly. "When you close how will I complete the sets of anniversary plates I started for my family?" Bernice and her husband Graham had celebrated their sixtieth wedding anniversary last month. A wall in their dining room was devoted to china plates commemorating each and every anniversary of their long marriage.

I had frequently contemplated discontinuing the anniversary plate line. The plates were getting hard to find, the selection marginal, and except for the Kellys, were in small demand. However, Bernice had been purchasing anniversary plates for the past thirty years, and now passed the tradition on to her extensive family. Every month or so she came into the store to buy a plate for one of her children who was celebrating a wedding milestone. Eight children times twenty-five plates equaled a lot of plates. And, now, the grandchildren were receiving the ubiquitous platters. With all the china on their walls, the Kellys could host a banquet for the city of Chandler.

Bernice selected a couple of plates for upcoming anniversaries and presented the coupon on the flyer that entitled her to an additional 10% discount beyond the 25% discount advertised during our first week of closeout.

Week Two:

"I'm sorry, Gus, we will not be able to refund your money on this desk lamp." I pointed to prominent signs posted throughout the store. *All sales final. No refunds or exchanges.*

"But, last week I only got 25% off on this lamp. This week I would get 40% off," Gus protested.

"And the lamp might not have been here for you to purchase this week," I countered and left Gus to stew in displeasure of this abrupt treatment.

Week Three:

"Compliments of Serrano's Restaurant." A full course Mexican dinner arrived at lunchtime. Platters of tacos, tamales, and enchiladas. Tubs of Spanish rice and refried beans. Baskets of corn chips and bowls of salsa. The staff feasted in shifts, for a crew had to remain on the floor to manage the throngs.

By week three, when discounts reached sixty percent, word of Chandler Stationers' closing had hit the airwaves. Long lines formed at the cash register, shopping carts and baskets heaped with gift items, party goods, and traditional office supplies. An unreal air of festivity permeated the store as old customers greeted one another and chatted amiably in the wake of the store's demise.

I found that I needed more help. I recruited assistance from friends in my P.E.O. chapter. As a fund raiser for the organization, members donated their time to wrap and box merchandise as it was sold. When the dust settled I would present the chapter with a donation check representing their wages. A win-win for all involved. The P.E.O. chapter earned a good bit of money for its philanthropic projects, and I would be able to take the donation as a tax write-off. With additional help at the check-out counter my clerks were free to provide assistance on the floor.

Week Four:

They say that in a lifetime everyone experiences fifteen minutes of fame. My fifteen minutes came in two-minute bursts. Press releases circulated among local television and radio stations. KPHO, KTVK and KAET production trucks rolled up to the front door. Cameramen hopped out and ran into the store, large cameras whirring on their shoulders. They captured lines queuing through the aisles, snaggle-toothed shelves, and empty racks spinning listlessly. Glamorous reporters checked their lipstick and ran combs through their hair before stepping in front of the cameras to conduct their interviews.

They pushed microphones under my nose.

"And why is an old established store like Chandler Stationers closing?" they asked.

"The nature of the office supply business has changed. It is time for me to throw in the towel," was my response.

They talked to my clerks.

"This has been a fun place to work. We have been at the center of everything going on in town."

They talked to my daughters.

"We've worked here off-and-on since we were ten years old."

They talked to the customers.

"I am heartbroken. This has always been the store where you could get hard-to-find-items."

A half-hour in the store documenting our disheveled

shelves and interviewing bargain-laden shoppers resulted in short spots across the six o'clock news.

Newspaper reporters descended. *The Arizona Republic* and *The Chandler Tribune* ran feature articles on their local pages – human interest stories that topped adopt-a-pet stories of last week. My picture was splashed above headlines *Piece of Chandler History to Close Doors*. Independent community publications jumped on the bandwagon. Ah, if only we could have had this kind of publicity when we were viably in business.

Wide-spread notoriety brought old acquaintances to the store to say goodbye. One evening after I locked the door behind a customer wielding a Santa-sized pack of merchandise, I heard a tap-tap-tapping on the pane. I had to squint to identify the face pressed against the glass.

"Tomás!" I gasped. I unlocked the door to admit Tomás, our premier stock boy of yore.

"I saw the story of the store's closing on the news last night," he said. "I drove down from Payson after work today to say goodbye." Tomás walked aimlessly through the aisles that he had kept so meticulously mopped. Dusty footprints formed erratic trails around the room. He ran his hand over topsy-turvy shelves of file folders that he had kept in scrupulous numerical order.

"Would you like for me to run a mop around the store?" he asked.

"No, Tomás." Weariness of the preceding weeks settled like lead weights around my shoulders. "It doesn't matter any more."

As the month rolled to a close, picked-over merchandise held little allure to savvy shoppers. Lines dwindled. When I closed the doors forever I planned to regroup, then I would bring in a liquidator to take the spoils.

On the last day of the month, near closing time, a taxi parked in front of the store. The driver got out and opened the back door. With great effort an old woman emerged. The taxi driver helped her unfold a walker then assisted her as she negotiated the high curb. The woman squared her shoulders and with considerable effort pushed the walker toward the entrance of the store. As she approached I could see that she would have trouble opening the door. I stepped forward to hold the door for her.

"Oh my goodness. Miss Arbuckle," I whispered.

Miss Arbuckle had been an old woman thirty years ago when I first met her, a kindly, vibrant woman nearing her seventh decade at the time. Good-natured laugh lines framed her twinkly blue eyes. In those days she pulled her thin gray hair back into a severe bun, but tendrils escaped giving her an appearance of whimsical disarray. She wore comfortable print housedresses and sensible old-lady lace-up shoes with thick heels. Miss Arbuckle seemed to be a woman content with her station in life. And she was pecking out her memoirs on a classic Underwood typewriter. She had come into Chandler Stationers regularly to purchase typewriter ribbon, paper, and correction fluid for her project.

Miss Arbuckle had spent a career teaching Indian children at BIA schools on the Navajo Reservation. Upon her retirement from teaching she moved to Chandler to be close to family. She spoke fondly of her life among the Navajos. She had undoubtedly been a good teacher.

Her life on the reservation encompassed pivotal points in 20th Century Native American history. Miss Arbuckle had lived among the *Diné* (the People) when the Indian Citizenship Act and the Nationality Act were being hashed out bestowing Native Americans with citizenship as well as voting rights. She had taught several young Navajo men who were inducted into World War II as Marine code talkers, young men who with their unbreakable code turned the tides of war in the Pacific to our favor. She lived on the Navajo Reservation when uranium was discovered and tribal members were sent to the mines unaware of contamination and health risks involved. Her memoir would be fascinating.

I hadn't seen Miss Arbuckle for over twenty-five

years. I didn't know if the book had been completed. In fact, I was surprised that Miss Arbuckle was still alive. But here she was. The frail visage before me must be nearing 100 years old.

"I couldn't let you close without saying goodbye," she said.

"Come in, Miss Arbuckle. Let me find you a chair." I ushered her into the store.

"No, dear, you are busy. I just wanted to pay one last visit to my favorite store." Her old seamed face radiated confidence and serenity. She seemed unfazed by the clutter and disarray around her.

"Many years ago I discovered this wonderful store tucked away back of the park," she continued. "I could always find everything I needed and used in my study and writing.

"But, here. I have something for you." Miss Arbuckle rummaged in her cavernous black bag. From its depths she pulled out a small tin box. *Secretarial Typewriter Ribbon; Air-Tight; Factory Fresh.* Gracious. How many of these twin-spooled ribbons had I sold Miss Arbuckle? The box itself was a treasure, a real collector's item.

"Look inside," she urged.

I pried the reluctant lid up. Carefully packed amid cotton balls was a fragment from an ancient vessel. A piece of white pottery decorated with black interlocking scrolls – exquisite artistry crafted with rudimentary tools.

"You were always interested in my life among the Indians," Miss Arbuckle continued. "I found this pot shard on the desert floor seventy-five years ago. It was made by a prehistoric potter. There is no beginning or end to his scrollwork design. I believe that he tells us that people are connected through the ages. It's for you, My Dear; I know you will treasure it."

"Oh, Miss Arbuckle . . ." Until this moment I had not had time to cry, but now, an acrid lump filled my throat. My eyes began to sting.

"Change is difficult. There's no doubt about it," she said. "I resisted change when I left the Navajo Reservation. But new opportunities were on the horizon. There will be new opportunities for you, too." This from a woman who could look back on a long life of joys as well as hardships.

"Tell me, Miss Arbuckle, did you finish your memoir?"

"Yes, I finished my memoir. I did not try to have it commercially published. I took the pages to a copy center and had ten copies made for my nieces and nephews. I wanted them to know what life was like on an Indian reservation seventy-five years ago. Everyone has a story to tell. And that was my story.

"But, I can't stay," she continued. "My taxi waits. It will take me back to the old folks' home in Scottsdale where my nephew has put me. I reside in a place convenient to him so he can check on me now and then." With a twinkle in her eye she added, "I am now writing a book about life in an old folks' home. I want my family to know about that, too."

I walked Miss Arbuckle out to the taxi. At the curb I gave her a gentle hug. She felt like a dandelion in my quick embrace.

"Goodbye, Miss Arbuckle. Thank you for coming. Your visit was a light at the end of a tunnel." I turned toward the door. The gold gild letters on the glass had crackled and chipped after thirty years.

Chandler Stationers
Purveyor of Office Supplies
and
Fine Gifts

A camera whirred. It caught me as I locked the door behind my last customer.

Some day *I* might write a memoir.

Made in the USA
San Bernardino, CA
11 March 2015